Beginning Th[eory]
for adults

The Grown-Up Approach to Music Theory

NATHANIEL GUNOD

CD recorded at Bar None Studio, Northford, CT
Cover photograph: Tim Becker/Creative Images Photography
Acoustic guitar on cover courtesy of Timothy Phelps
Violin on cover courtesy of Emily Flower
Flute on cover courtesy of Nicole Stevenson
"Jake" (golden retriever) courtesy of Mark Dutton
Special thanks to Mr. and Mrs. Fontana for the use of their home.

Alfred Music Publishing Co., Inc.
P.O. Box 10003
Van Nuys, CA 91410-0003
alfred.com

ISBN-10: 0-7390-9306-1 (Book & CD)
ISBN-13: 978-0-7390-9306-1 (Book & CD)

 Alfred Cares. Contents printed on 100% recycled paper.

Contents

Beginning Theory for Adults

Contents

Introduction

For some reason, learning to read and understand music seems scary to lots of adults. We are sometimes reluctant to learn new things. A person who has been a successful parent, or successfully earned a living for some time, may feel intimidated by things they don't know well. We feel it may be tough going back to being a student.

If you have always wanted to express yourself musically, but are experiencing reservations like those described above, this book is for you. It was written specifically with you in mind. The idea behind it is to keep this learning process easy and enjoyable.

Of course, just reading this book, listening to the CD and completing the exercises won't be enough. You need a good teacher who will be sensitive to your particular combination of excitement and/or fear when it comes to learning to play music. You need to feel very comfortable with this person because, despite all you have accomplished in life so far, you are going to have to let them help you take baby steps.

You may fear that things that the pros make look easy to do may make you feel foolish when you try them the first time. But remember—there is nothing foolish about learning to make music. You should be congratulated for finally getting started learning to play. You are very courageous, and the rewards will be fulfilling beyond your hopes and expectations. All you need is to have patience and stick-to-it-ive-ness. Nothing this good comes fast and easy.

This book is not about teaching your fingers to play your chosen instrument. It is about understanding what your fingers will play, learning to hear important musical elements and discerning between differences within them. Learning this material will add meaning to the sounds you are learning to make. It will add meaning to the music you love to listen to. It will get you started down the road of being a musician.

Because of its visual clarity, the piano keyboard is used to explain many ideas in this book. The guitar, however, is also a very popular instrument that we know many of our readers are learning to play. For that reason, you will find gray boxes with information specifically for guitarists that begin like this: **Note for Guitarists.** Guitarists will find some special worksheet problems in these spots too. But guitarists should read all of the information and do all of the worksheets, not just those marked especially for guitarists. The "Note for Guitarists" boxes are additional information and work for guitarists, not substitutes for the rest.

This is just a beginning book, and you will need to learn lots more than what is between these covers, but we all have to start somewhere. Thanks for choosing this place to start. I hope you will have a great time, and that music remains an important part of the rest of your life.

Enjoy!

About the CD
This book includes numerous ear training exercises and is thus accompanied by a CD. Every ear training exercise is indicated with the symbol shown to the right, which will tell which CD track applies. The CD includes plenty of demonstrations to make it easy for you to hear the concepts being studied.

Track
#

Chapter One

lesson 1: what is music?

Vocabulary this page:
music/pitch/frequency/rhythm/beats

A dictionary definition of music might be "the art of ordering sounds and silences in succession over time to produce a composition having unity and continuity." There's truth there, but it's a bit dry. Especially nowadays, when we are forced to throw everything from the compositions of Bach and Beethoven to atonal contemporary "classical" music , pop and rap into one big pot and call it, collectively, "music."

Like it or not, there are common elements between all of these. In this book, we will be dealing with the most fundamental building blocks for any musical style: pitch and musical time.

Pitch

In the broadest musical sense, pitch is the degree of highness or lowness of a sound. Every sound in a musical composition has pitch as one of its features; even the percussive ones, like the beat of a drum or the scratch of a DJ's turntable. There is a scientific way to measure pitch. A regularly vibrating object will create sound waves that have a frequency or speed at which the vibrations occur. The faster the vibrations, the higher sounding the pitch; the slower the vibrations, the lower sounding the pitch. If you ever go to hear a symphony orchestra perform, probably the first thing that will happen is the oboe player will play an A 440, which is a pitch whose sound waves, if measured, would have a frequency of 440 cycles per second. The rest of the orchestra "tunes" to this note.

faster = higher
slower = lower

Surely you have observed that some instruments, like the flute or violin, make higher sounds, and others, such as the tuba or bass, make lower sounds. The piano has a very wide range, from very low to very high, and the guitar, by comparison, is mostly a low-sounding instrument, although it can play some medium-high sounds.

Being able to discern pitch—to know which notes are higher and which notes are lower—is part of learning music.

Time

A painting happens on a canvas, a sculpture in stone. Music happens in time. A song or piece will begin at one time, and end some time later. How the pitches (and silences) are organized in time is one of the most important aspects of music. There are long sounds and very fast sounds. This is one of the elements that distinguishes one moment of music from another, or one piece from another.

Long and short sounds most often are presented in a very clear pattern that is very recognizable. For example, think about the tune, Jingle Bells: If you heard someone clapping the pattern of short-short-long, short-short-long that we hear on the words "Jin-gle Bells, Jin-gle Bells," you would immediately know it was the song Jingle Bells. That pattern of long and short is called a rhythm. Rhythms happen against a grid of musical pulses called beats. Without a steady stream of beats against which to play rhythms, rhythms would be impossible to recognize.

ie. 44?

lesson 2: the musical alphabet
and reading pitch (treble)

Vocabulary this page:
notes/note heads/stems/flags/beams/staff

Music, as much as anything else, is about communication. It is its nature to communicate via sound. But one musician must be able to communicate to another anywhere else in the world how music should sound. So music is also a written language. Somehow, this is one of the things that some adults find the most intimidating about learning to play music. This is understandable because as adults, we are no longer in the "language acquisition" stage in our lives. That's for babies. Our brains are not made for it, and we know it.

But that doesn't mean we can't learn. When we travel to a different country, we can learn to read some signs and restaurant menus. The natives are generally patient with us if we try. So, too, will your teacher help you navigate the language of music. And this book will help you as well. Fear not.

Notes

Musical pitches (pitch is the highness or lowness of a sound) are represented with notes, which are symbols made with a combination of *heads*, *stems*, *flags* and *beams*.

The Parts of Notes

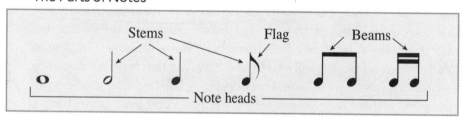

They are placed on or around a *staff*, which is a group five lines and the spaces between them. These lines are numbered from the bottom up.

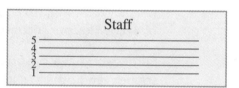

The higher a note is placed on the staff, the higher its pitch.

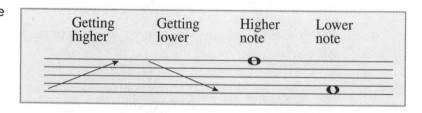

The Musical Alphabet

Like any language, music has an alphabet. The musical alphabet contains seven letters: A B C D E F and G. This alphabet is repeated as needed to represent lower and higher notes. As you go forward in the alphabet, notes get higher in pitch. For example, B sounds higher than A, unless of course, the A comes later in the alphabet.

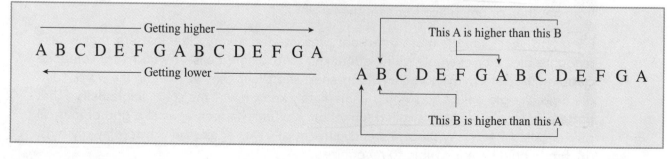

Vocabulary this page:
clef/ treble clef/G clef/ treble staff

At the beginning of every staff is a clef. A clef is a sign that organizes the staff, telling us which pitches are represented by placing notes on which lines or spaces. There are various kinds of clefs. For higher sounding notes, the treble clef is used.

This is the treble clef:

Treble clef is also called G clef because it developed over the centuries from the letter G, and its curl surrounds the G line on the staff:

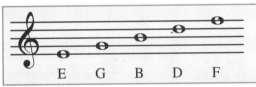

By relating everything to the G line, we can know the names of all the other lines and spaces on the treble staff (a staff with a treble clef).

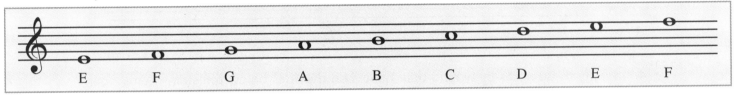

On the treble staff, the notes on the lines are (from bottom to top): E, G, B, D, F. You can remember this with the phrase: **E**very **G**ood **B**oy **D**oes **F**ine.

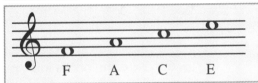

On the treble staff, the notes in the spaces are: F, A, C, E. It is helpful to remember that these letters spell the word FACE.

David is from Sydney, Australia. He started playing drums at the age of 7, and guitar at 10. About 20 years ago, he came back to music and he says, "Apart from my wife, my guitar is my best friend. Music breaks down language and cultural barriers. It is a universal language."

Exercises

1. In each example of this exercise, you will be played two notes. If the second note is higher, circle the word "Higher." If the second note is lower, circle the word "Lower."

   A. Lower (Higher)   B. Lower (Higher)   C. Lower (Higher)   D. Lower Higher

2. Which example is the rhythm to "Jingle Bells?"

   A.   (B.)   C.   D.

3. Write a line of eight treble clefs in three steps as shown.

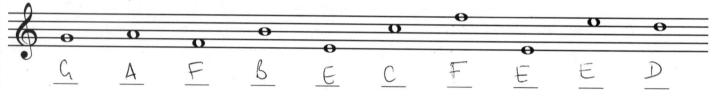

4. Identify these notes by writing their names on the lines below the staff. Remember Every Good Boy Does Fine, FACE and that you can use the G line, circled by the clef, as a point of reference.

   G   A   F   B   E   C   F   E   E   D

5. Write the notes indicated below the staff. If the note can be written in two different locations, show both.

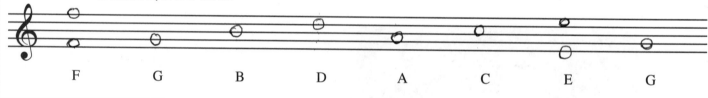

   F   G   B   D   A   C   E   G

Charles Hurt, 51
Nuclear Specialist

From Baxley, Georgia, Charles is a Nuclear Specialist at a nuclear power plant. He started playing piano in the 3rd grade. Charles says, "Music is my life pleasure and hobby. I want to better understand what I play, which is why I study theory."

Beginning Theory for Adults

lesson 3: reading pitch (bass)

Vocabulary this page:
bass clef/F clef/bass staff/staves/brace/grand staff

For lower sounding notes, the bass clef is used.

This is the bass clef: 𝄢

Bass clef is also called F clef because it developed over the centuries from the letter F, and its dots surround the F line on the staff:

By relating everything to the F line, we can know the names of all the other lines and spaces on the bass staff (a staff with a bass clef).

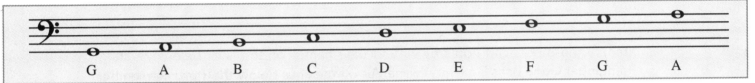

On the bass staff, the notes on the lines are (from bottom to top): G, B, D, F, A. You can remember this with the phrase: **G**ood **B**oys **D**o **F**ine **A**lways.

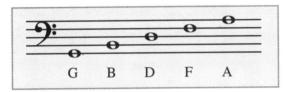

On the bass staff, the notes in the spaces are: A, C, E, G. You can remember this with the phrase: **A**ll **C**ows **E**at **G**rass.

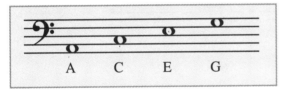

lesson 4: the grand staff

Many instruments need just one staff: violin, flute, guitar (treble); string bass, tuba, electric bass (bass). Piano music is written with two clefs. The right-hand part (higher notes) is written on a treble staff; the left-hand part is written on a bass staff. The two staves (plural for staff) are connected with a brace and a line to become a grand staff.

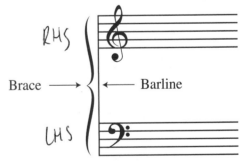

Here are all the notes on lines and spaces of the grand staff.

Chapter One

Exercises

Track 3

1. Which examples have ascending notes (notes getting higher)? Which examples have descending notes (notes getting lower)? Circle the answer for each of the four.

   A. Ascending (Descending)   B. (Ascending) Descending

   C. (Ascending) Descending   D. Ascending (Descending)

2. Draw a line of eight bass clefs. Make one stroke and then surround F, fourth line, with two dots, as shown.

3. Identify these bass clef notes by writing their names on the lines below the staff. Remember Good Boys Do Fine Always, All Cows Eat Grass and that you can use the F line, surrounded by the dots of the clef, as a point of reference.

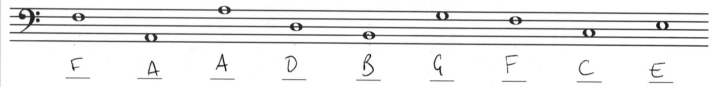

   F   A   A   D   B   G   F   C   E

4. Write the notes indicated below the staff. If the note can be written in two different locations, show both.

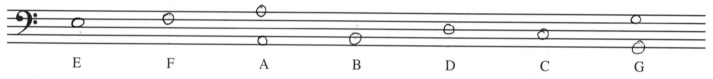

   E   F   A   B   D   C   G

5. Identify these notes. Pay attention to the changing clefs.

   G   C   B   D   F   E   D   B   G   E   F

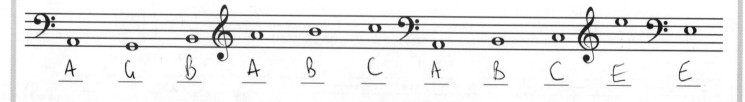

   A   G   B   A   B   C   A   B   C   E   E

Chapter Two

lesson 1: note values

Vocabulary this page:
note value/whole note/half note/quarter note

As discussed on page 5, music is created with pitch and rhythms. A rhythm is a pattern created with long and short sounds. The duration of a note is the note's value. The first note values we will discuss are whole notes, half notes and quarter notes.

These note values are symbolized through the use of different note heads, and the presence or absence of stems (see page 6 for a review of the parts of notes).

Here are what whole notes, half notes and quarter notes look like:

Whole Notes

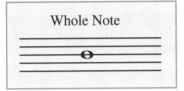

Half Notes

Below the third line of the staff, the stems go up from the right.

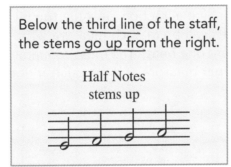

On or above the third line of the staff, the stems go down from the left.

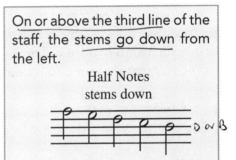

Quarter Notes

Below the third line of the staff, the stems go up from the right.

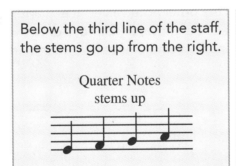

On or above the third line of the staff, the stems go down from the left.

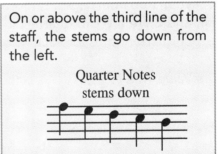

Of these three note values, the whole note is the longest. As you might guess from thinking about their names, the half note is half the length of a whole note, and the quarter note is one-fourth the length of a whole note. So, the time of two half notes equals the time of one whole note. Likewise, the time of two quarter notes equals the time of one half note. The time of four quarter notes equals the time of one whole note.

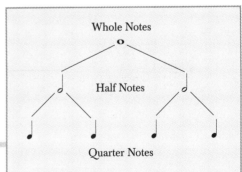

Exercises

The answers to these three arithmetic problems are all note values. Draw quarter notes, half notes or whole notes.

1. ♩ + ♩ = 𝅗𝅥

2. ♩ + ♩ + ♩ + ♩ = 𝅝

3. 𝅗𝅥 + 𝅗𝅥 = 𝅝

4. 𝅝 − 𝅗𝅥 = 𝅗𝅥

lesson 2: measures and time signatures

Vocabulary this page:
measure/bar lines/time signature

The time in a piece of music is counted in beats (page 5), which are the basic unit of measure in musical time. The steady pulse of the beats is the glue that holds the music together. It is the grid against which rhythms are performed and understood. When you tap your foot to music, you are tapping the beats.

A given piece may have hundreds or even thousands of beats. These beats are organized into groups called measures. Measures are marked in written music with bar lines.

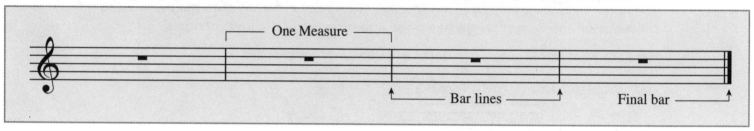

A time signature is a sign at the beginning of a piece to the right of the clef. It contains two numbers, one on top of the other, like a fraction. It is the top number of the time signature that tells us how many beats will be in each measure. The bottom number tells us which kind of note will represent one beat. The most common time signature is 4/4 It tells us that there are four beats per measure and the quarter note gets one beat.

(handwritten: what represents a beat? beats)

4 Four beats per measure
4 The quarter note ♩ gets one beat

Now that we know that the quarter note equals one beat, we can use simple logic, and the rhythm tree from page 11, to learn the other note values. If a quarter note equals one beat, and there are two quarters in each half note, a half note gets two beats. If there are four quarter notes for each whole note, a whole note lasts four beats.

Note Value Tree in 4/4

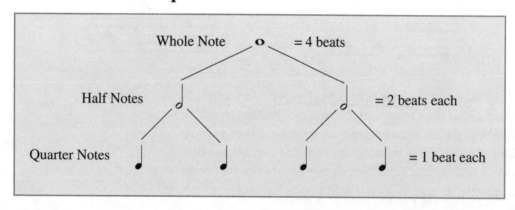

Exercises

1. The answers to these problems will be numbers.

   A. ♩ + ♩ = __1/2__

   B. ♩ + ♩ = __1__

   C. ♩ + ♩ = __3/4__

2. What does this time signature mean?

   3 = A. __Three__ beats per measure
   4 = B. The __quarter__ note gets one beat

3. Which measure has too many beats? Circle it.

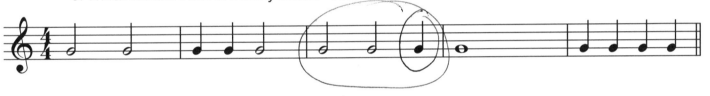

4. Use quarter notes to complete the incomplete measures.

lesson 3: rests (whole/half/quarter)

Vocabulary this page:
whole rest/half rest/quarter rest

Silence is a very important part of music. Rests help to separate musical ideas. They can create a feeling of relaxation, or even tension, in music. They allow wind players and singers to breathe. The list goes on.

Every note value has a corresponding rest. Here are the note values you have learned so far and their corresponding rests.

Notice that the whole rest hangs from the second line and the half rest sits on the third line. The quarter rest makes many people think of a bird flying sideways.

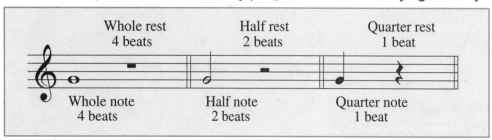

Whole rest	Half rest	Quarter rest
4 beats	2 beats	1 beat
Whole note	Half note	Quarter note
4 beats	2 beats	1 beat

Exercises

1. The answers to the following problems are numbers.

   A. — + — = _1_

   B. 𝄽 + — = _3/4_

   C. — + 𝄽 = _1¼_

2. Circle the measures with too many beats.

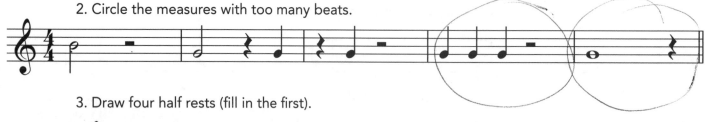

3. Draw four half rests (fill in the first).

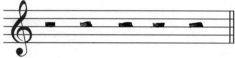

4. Draw four whole rests (fill in the first).

5. Draw four quarter rests (connect the dots to draw the first).

lesson 4: ties and slurs

Vocabulary this page:
tie/slur/hammer-on/pull-off

Ties

You may be wondering, "what if a note is longer than four beats?" This is a perfectly logical question with an easy answer. The answer is that it is tied to another note. A tie joins the values of two notes of the same pitch. The first note in a tie is played or sung, but not the second. The value of the second note, the tied note, is added to that of the first.

[handwritten: different to a slur? yes!]

For example, if a G whole note (four beats) is tied to a G half note (two beats), it is held for six beats.

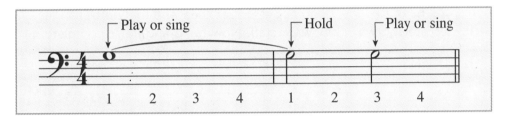

Slurs

A *slur* connects two notes of different pitches, indicating that they should be very smoothly connected. It does not change a note's value. It is important not to confuse a tie with a slur.

Exercises

[handwritten: ○ = 4 beats]

The answers to these problems are numbers:

[handwritten: ○ = 1]

1. ○ ⌣ 𝅗𝅥 = __6__   *[handwritten: 1½]*

2. 𝅗𝅥 ⌣ ♩ = __3__   *[handwritten: 3/4]*

3. ♩ ⌣ ♩ = __2__   *[handwritten: ½]*

4. ○ ⌣ ♩ = __5__   *[handwritten: 1¼]*

> **NOTE FOR GUITARISTS**
>
> A slur between ascending notes indicates a *hammer-on*. Pluck the first note with the right hand but let the left-hand finger sound the next. A slur between descending notes is a *pull-off*. Pluck the first note but remove the left-hand finger to let the note held by a lower finger sound.

Chapter Three

lesson 1: ledger lines

Vocabulary this page:
ledger lines

Some notes are too high or too low to be written on the staff. In those cases, *ledger lines* are used. A ledger line is a short line used to extend the staff either higher or lower.

You may have noticed that some notes were missing from the grand staff shown on page 9. To fill in the missing notes, you need to understand about ledger lines, and that notes can be written in the spaces immediately above or below the staff. Now, our grand staff is complete.

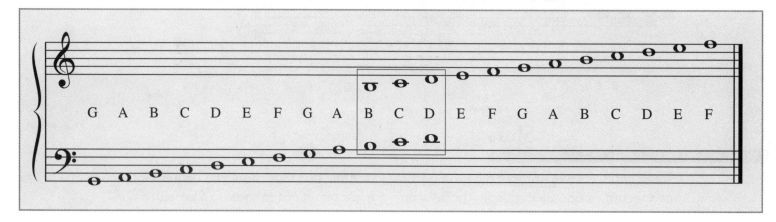

The ledger lines can also be used to write much higher notes.

The ledger lines can also be used to write much lower notes.

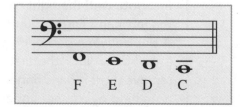

Exercises

1. Write the names of the treble staff notes on the lines beneath the staff.

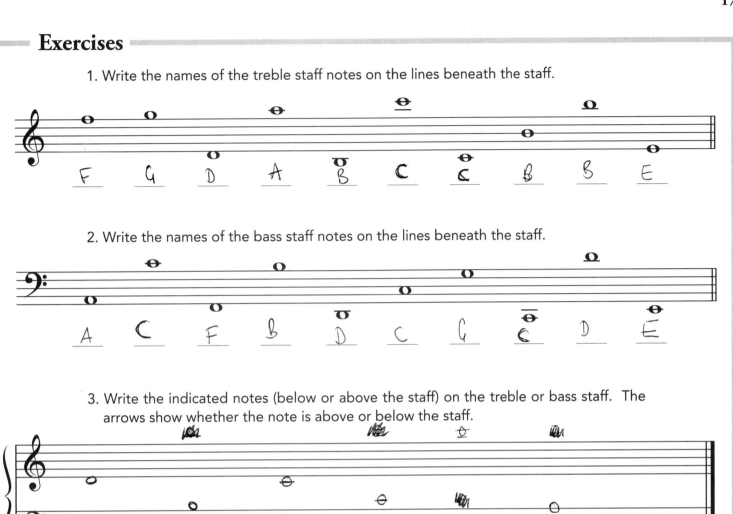

F G D A B C C B B E

2. Write the names of the bass staff notes on the lines beneath the staff.

A C F B D C G C D E

3. Write the indicated notes (below or above the staff) on the treble or bass staff. The arrows show whether the note is above or below the staff.

D↓ 𝄢 B↑ C↓ 𝄢 C↑ C↑ A↓ 𝄢 C↓

Tom Weaver, 48
Substance Abuse Counselor

A substance abuse counselor from Maryland, Tom has been playing guitar for 20 years. He says, "Studying theory opens up a new world. It gives you the mechanics you need to be more creative." In a more reflective mode, he says, "Music is where I find my spirituality."

Chapter Three

lesson 2: close and far

One of the most important things to understand about music is the relationship between pitches. Some pitches are very close together, and some are very far apart. As you learned on page 6, music notation is not only symbolic, but it is representative, too.

In other words, pitches that are high, look high. Pitches that are low, look low.

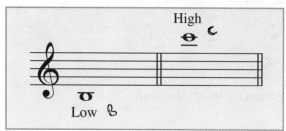

It's the same with pitch relationships; pitches that are close together, generally look close together. Pitches that are far apart, generally look far apart.

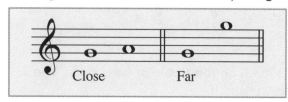

But it's important to keep clefs in mind. When we compare notes in two different clefs, they may look deceivingly close.

Unless they are on a grand staff.

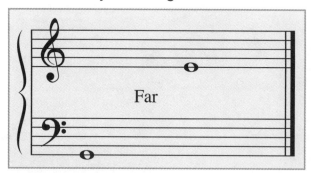

Exercises

1. Do these pairs of notes look close to each other, or far apart? Circle the answer underneath each.

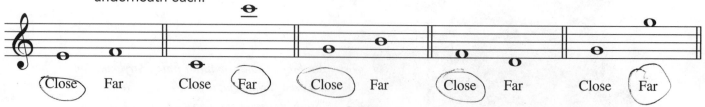

2. You will hear four pairs of notes on the CD, A–D. Listen and decide whether they sound close to each other, or far apart. Circle the correct answer for each.

Track 4

A. Close (Far)   B. (Close) Far   C. (Close) Far   D. Close (Far)

lesson 3: whole steps and half steps

Vocabulary this page:
whole steps/half steps/fret/fretboard

The distance between notes can be measured in steps. A *step* is the distance between two notes that are adjacent in the musical alphabet. A step is a close distance.

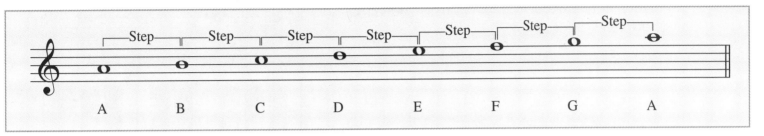

Whole Steps

There are two kinds of steps. On the piano, a *whole step* is the distance between two white keys that have one black key between them. The distance between two black keys that have one white key between them is also a whole step. The keys that are marked in the diagram show that any two keys that have one other key between them are whole steps.

because of semitones!

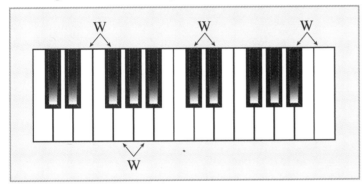

NOTE FOR GUITARISTS

On a guitar, a whole step is the distance of two frets, with no other frets between them. (Frets are the metal wires that divide the fretboard, which is the playing area of the neck of a fretted, stringed instrument.) Any two frets separated by one fret is a whole step. Also, the distance of an open string to the 2nd fret is a whole step.

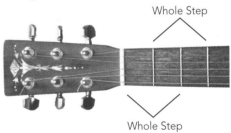

On a guitar, a half step is the distance between any two adjacent frets. Also, the distance from the open string to the 1st fret is a half step.

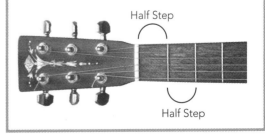

Half Steps

On a piano, a *half step* is the distance between any two adjacent keys that have no other keys between them.

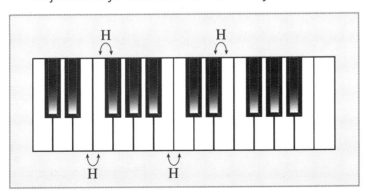

lesson 4: the musical alphabet and whole and half steps

Let's look at the musical alphabet on the keyboard and observe the whole steps and half steps. This will illustrate a very important fact that you should memorize: There is a whole step between every note in the musical alphabet except between E & F and B & C.

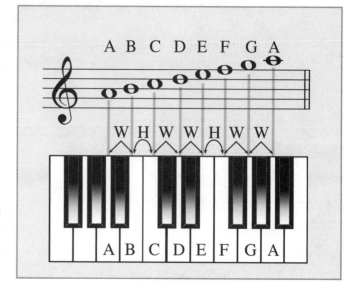

This is why the keyboard is designed the way it is, with repeating patterns of groups of three black and two black keys. This visual organization of white and black keys (as whole steps and half steps affect it) is what makes the keyboard such an indispensable tool for all musicians when learning theory.

NOTE FOR GUITARISTS

The musical alphabet has the same organization of whole steps and half steps on every instrument. It has never, however, affected the overall design of the guitar. Looking at the notes of the musical alphabet along one string makes it easy to see the whole steps and half steps.

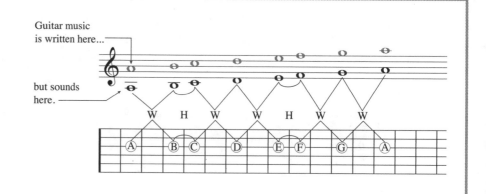

Exercises

1. Identify the steps shown the keyboard below. Use W for whole steps, and H for half steps.

Track 5

2. You will hear two notes. Is the second note a half step higher, or a whole step higher? Circle the W if it's a whole step. Circle the H if it's a half step.

A. (W) H   B. W (H)   C. W (H)   D. (W) H

Track 6

3. You will hear two notes. Is the second note a half step lower, or a whole step lower? Circle the W if it's a whole step. Circle the H if it's a half step.

A. W H   B. W H   C. W H   D. W H

EXERCISE FOR GUITARISTS

Identify the steps shown on the fretboard diagram below. Use W for whole steps, and H for half steps.

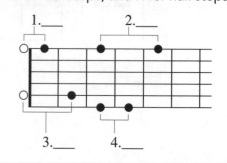

lesson 5: accidentals

Vocabulary this page:
accidental/flat

An accidental is a sign that alters the pitch of a note by making it higher or lower, or returning it to its original pitch.

The Flat ♭

When a flat sign is placed directly before a note, the pitch is lowered by one half step. When we talk about a flatted note, the letter name of the note comes first. For example, if a flat is placed before an A, it is called "A-flat."

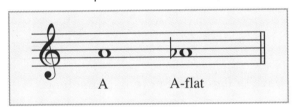

The flat should always appear directly on the space or line of the note it is affecting.

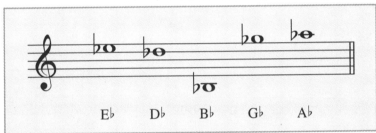

To flat a note on the keyboard, play the next lower key, whether it is black or white.

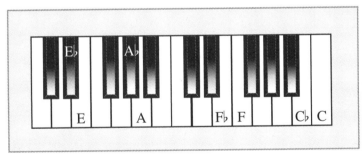

The Sharp ♯

When a sharp sign is placed directly before a note, the pitch is raised by one half step. When we talk about a sharped note, the letter name of the note comes first. For example, if a sharp is placed before a G, it is called "G-sharp."

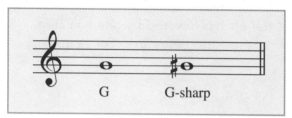

The sharp should always appear directly on the space or line of the note it is affecting.

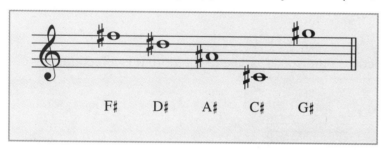

To sharp a note on the keyboard, play the next higher key, whether it is black or white.

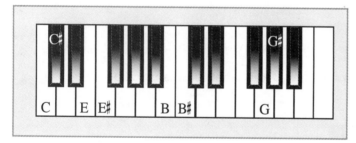

The Natural ♮

When a natural sign is placed directly before a note, it cancels out a previous flat or sharp. When we talk about a natural note, the letter name of the note comes first. For example, if a natural is placed before a C, it is called "C-natural." On a keyboard, a natural is always a white key.

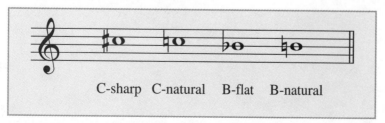

NOTE FOR GUITARISTS

To flat a note, play it on the next lower fret. To sharp a note, play it on the next higher fret. To flat a note on an open string, find it on the next lower string and then lower it one fret. To sharp a note on an open string, play it on the 1st fret.

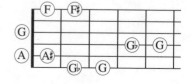

Beginning Theory for Adults

lesson 6: accidentals and measures

When a flat or sharp is placed in front of a note, that note remains flat or sharp for the duration of the measure. In the next measure, the accidental no longer has any affect, unless the note is tied.

When a flat or sharp is placed in front of a note, an accidental is required to return that note to its original pitch during the measure, or in the next measure if it was flat or sharp and then tied into the measure.

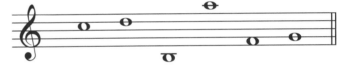

Exercises

To draw a flat sign, first draw one vertical line. Then draw a heavy curved line to form a half circle. To keep it from looking like a lowercase "b," make the half circle more slender at the bottom.

1. Draw flats in front of these notes.

To draw a sharp, first draw two parallel thin vertical lines. Then add the slanted, heavier lines.

2. Draw sharps in front of these notes.

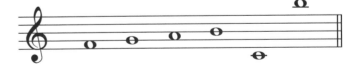

To draw a natural sign, first draw the left half (a vertical line with a slanted line at the bottom). Then draw the right half (a lower, parallel vertical line with a slanted line at the top).

3. Draw naturals in front of these notes.

4. Write the names of the notes on the lines under the staff.

Chapter Four

lesson 1: octaves and the chromatic scale

Vocabulary this page:
octave/scale/chromatic scale

An *octave* is the closest distance between any two notes with the same name. This is always a distance of 12 half steps, which is considered to be a far distance between notes.

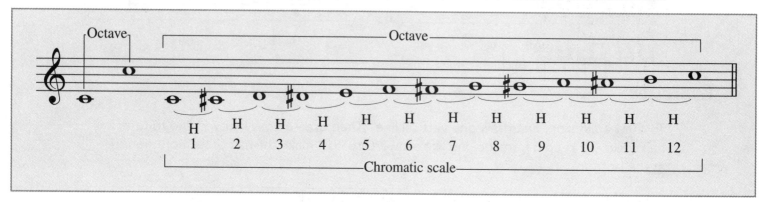

If you played every half step between the two notes in an octave, you would be playing the *chromatic scale*. A scale is a series of pitches, in alphabetical order, with a specific arrangement of steps.

Joe has a degree in Psychology and teaches guitar to children and adults in Nanuet, NY. He says, "Studying music theory reveals parts of yourself that you wouldn't otherwise know exists. Life begins again when you start studying music as an adult."

lesson 2: enharmonic equivalents
and the chromatic scale

Vocabulary this page:
enharmonic equivalents/enharmonic tones

Any sharp note can also have a flat name. Any flat note can also have a sharp name. When two pitches sound the same but have different names, they are said to be *enharmonically equivalent.*

On the keyboard, for example, the black key just above a C is called C-sharp. The black key just below a D is called D-flat. In both cases, the same black key is played. C-sharp is the *enharmonic tone* of D-flat, and vice-verse.

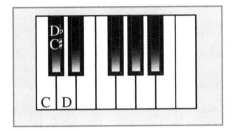

Below is the chromatic scale you learned in Lesson 1 at the top of the page, but this time, descending. Notice that when descending, the accidentals are expressed as flats instead of sharps. This is the common practice: when ascending, use sharps; when descending, use flats. To help clarify the concept, the enharmonic note names are shown below the notes with accidentals.

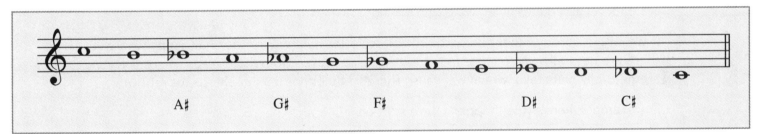

A♯   G♯   F♯   D♯   C♯

NOTE FOR GUITARISTS

On the guitar fretboard, it works similarly. The C on the 2nd string is at the 1st fret. C-sharp is at the 2nd fret. D is at the 3rd fret. D-flat is at the 2nd fret. The 2nd fret is both C-sharp and D-flat; these two pitches are enharmonically related.

Chapter Four

lesson 3: the major scale

Vocabulary this page:
major scale/tonic/keynote/scale formula

As you learned on page 24, a scale is a series of pitches, in alphabetical order, with a specific arrangement of steps. The most important scale in the music of the Western world is the major scale. It is the basis for many concepts that will follow in your study of music, so learn it well.

The specific arrangement of whole steps and half steps in the major scale is as follows:

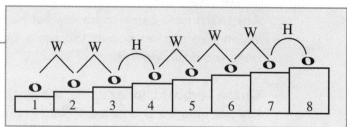

Let's build this scale starting on the note C. The note from which a major scale is built is called the tonic (or sometimes, the keynote). Notice that the scale spans an octave; it ends on the tonic, one octave above where we started.

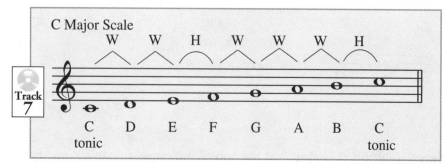

The scale is named after the tonic. The scale above is called the "C Major scale." The C Major scale is the only major scale that has no sharps and flats. This is because the musical alphabet already has half steps between E & F and B & C, which is what the specific arrangement of whole steps and half steps in the major scale (which we will call the major scale formula) requires when we begin a major scale on C.

If we begin on any other tonic, the major scale formula will call for half steps where there are naturally whole steps in the musical alphabet, or for whole steps where there are naturally half steps, which will cause there to be either flats or sharps (never both).

For example, here's what happens if we start on a G tonic:

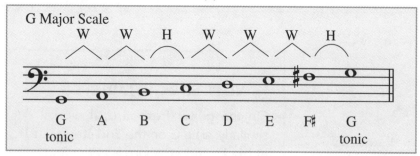

Since E to F is naturally a half step, to create a whole step we must change the F to F-sharp (F♯). We always change the next note as we progress through the musical alphabet, applying the scale formula.

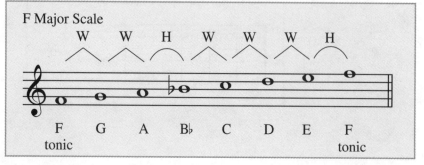

lesson 4: tetrachords

Vocabulary this page:
tetra/tetrachord

Tetra is a very old word (Latin/Greek) meaning "four." A tetrachord is a group of four pitches arranged in stepwise, alphabetical order. A major tetrachord has the following formula:

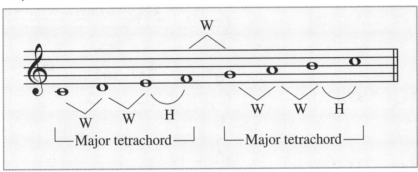

If you observe the first four notes and the last four notes of the major scale, you will see that they are both major tetrachords. A major scale is two major tetrachords with a whole step between them.

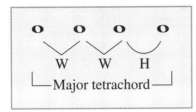

Ear Training Exercises

Track 8

1. On the CD, you will hear four scales. Indicate whether it is chromatic or major by circling the correct answer.

   A. Major Chromatic   B. Major Chromatic   C. Major Chromatic   D. Major Chromatic

Track 9

2. On the CD, you will hear six scales. Indicate whether it is chromatic, major, or some other scale by circling the correct answer.

   A. Major Chromatic Other   B. Major Chromatic Other   C. Major Chromatic Other
   D. Major Chromatic Other   E. Major Chromatic Other   F. Major Chromatic Other

Track 10

3. Below are four melodic patterns made from major tetrachords, labeled 1, 2, 3 and 4. Which one of them are you hearing in examples A–H? Circle the answers.

   A. 1 2 3 4   B. 1 2 3 4   C. 1 2 3 4   D. 1 2 3 4
   E. 1 2 3 4   F. 1 2 3 4   G. 1 2 3 4   H. 1 2 3 4

Written Exercises

1. Write major tetrachords from the following notes:

A.   B.   C.   D.

2. Draw lines to match the bottom tetrachords of three major scales to their upper tetrachords. Remember, the two tetrachords that make up a major scale are separated by one whole step.

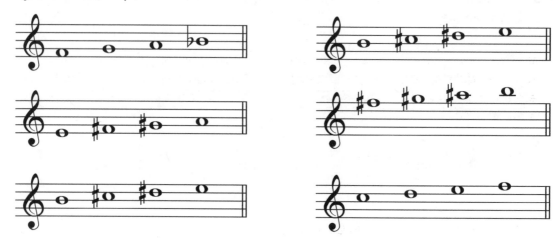

3. Use sharps or flats (never both) to change these scales to major scales. Don't change the tonic notes. Pay attention to the clefs.

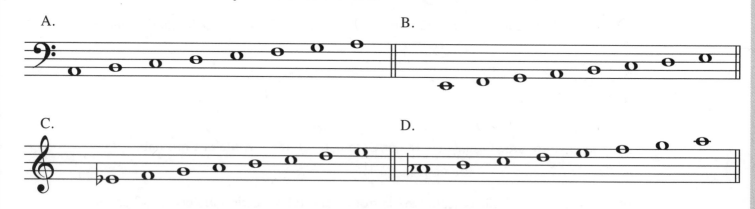

A.   B.

C.   D.

4. Write the names of the notes on the lines underneath the staff. Then, using sharps or flats where necessary, draw their enharmonic equivalents on the staff and write their names on the lines underneath the staff.

Chapter Five

lesson 1: eighth notes and rests

Vocabulary this page:
eighth note/flag/beam/eighth rest

On page 12, you learned the note value tree in $\frac{4}{4}$. You know that when there is a 4 on the bottom of a key signature, a quarter note equals one beat. If a quarter note equals one beat, then a half note equals two and a whole note equals four. As a quick review, he re is that note value tree again.

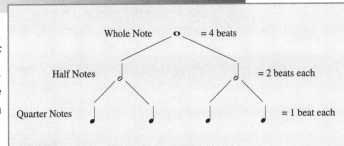

Just as we halve the value of a whole note to get half notes, and halve the value of a half note to get quarter notes, we can halve the value of a quarter note to get eighth notes. There are two eighth notes for each quarter note. So, in $\frac{4}{4}$ time, an eighth note equals one half of a beat.

A single eighth note has a flag and looks like this:

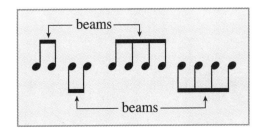

Eighth notes can be grouped in groups of two or four with beams.

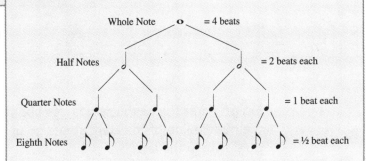

If there are two eighth notes for each quarter note, there are four eighth notes for each half note, and eight eighth notes for each whole note.

Here is an updated version of the note value tree, this time including eighth notes.

An eighth rest looks like this: ♪

For the sake of review, here is a rest value tree.

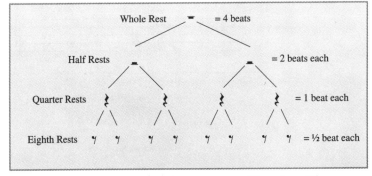

lesson 2: counting eighth notes and rests

Vocabulary this page:
on-beat/off-beat/subdividing

One helpful way to think about eighth notes and how they divide a beat into two parts is to think about tapping your foot, as you may sometimes do when listening to music. Each tap has two parts: 1) when your toes are on the ground, and 2) when they are in the air. Your toes are on the ground on the first part of the beat; let's call this the *on-beat*. They are in the air on the second part of the beat; let's call this the *off-beat*.

When counting eighth notes, we want to verbally divide each beat (called *subdividing*) using "and" (in this book, symbolized like this: &). For example, a measure of $\frac{4}{4}$ would be counted like this: "1-&, 2-&, 3-&, 4-&." The numbers are the on-beats; the "&s" are the off-beats.

Here are two examples with counting underneath. Try to count aloud and clap the rhythm. Hold your hands together on longer notes, take your hands apart on rests. Notice that it is recommended to start subdividing a beat or so before we actually perform eighth notes.

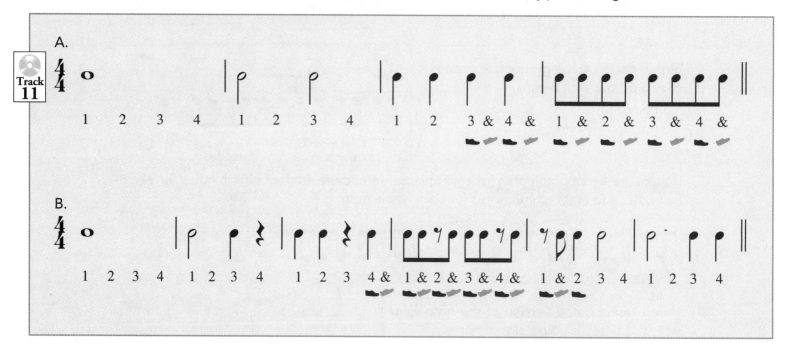

Eighth notes follow the same rules about stems as half notes and quarter notes. Below the middle line of the staff, stems go up on the right; on or above the third line, stems go down on the left.

Exercises

1. This is a melody by Johann Sebastian Bach (1685-1750). Write the counting underneath the music. You can write a plus sign (+) instead of ampersands (&). Be sure to align your counting with the correct notes.

2. Add stems, flags and beams as necessary to make these eighth notes. Remember the stems rule.

3. Complete the incomplete measures with beamed eighth notes. Remember this important rule: Never beam eighth notes from beat 2 to beat 3. This keeps the midpoint of the measure easy to see.

1 2   2 3 4 1   3   1   4   3 4

4. Add the values (in beats) of the notes and write the sums after the equal signs.

A. ♩ ♫♫ = _____

B. ♩ ♫ = _____

C. o ♫♫ = _____

D. ♩ ♩ ♫ = _____

Chapter Five

lesson 3: dotted half notes

Vocabulary this page:
dot/dotted note

As you learned on page 15, one way to extend the value of a note is to tie it to another note of the same pitch. Another way is to add a dot to the right of a note. When a dot is added to the right of a note, its value is increased by one half. For example:

A half note equals two beats.

$$\text{♩} = 2$$

Half of a half note is one beat (a quarter note).

$$\text{♩} = 1$$
$$\text{·} = 1$$

Two beats plus one beat equals three beats. A dotted half note equals three beats.

$$\text{♩} + \text{·} = \text{♩·}$$
$$2 + 1 = 3$$

It is also helpful to think of the dotted half note as being equal to a half note tied to a quarter note of the same pitch. In other words: In general, a dotted note is equal to the note's value tied to a note one step lower in the note value tree (page 29).

$$\text{♩·} = \text{♩}\smile\text{♩}$$

You can also dot a half rest to signify three beats of silence.

Dotted half rest

Three beats of silence

Exercises

To the right of the equal sign, write one note or rest equal to the value of the notes or rests to the left of the equal sign.

1. ♩· + ♩ = _____

2. ♩ + ♩ = _____

3. 𝄽 + ▬ = _____

4. 𝄿 + 𝄿 + ▬· = _____

lesson 4: $\frac{3}{4}$ time

So far in this book, we have dealt exclusively with $\frac{4}{4}$ time—four beats per measure and the quarter note equals one beat.

Let's look at $\frac{3}{4}$ time.
3 = Three beats per measure
4 = The quarter note still gets one beat.

Here is a sample of $\frac{3}{4}$ time. It is from a minuet by J. S. Bach. Minuets are usually in $\frac{3}{4}$. Notice the use of a final double bar—one thick bar line and one thin—to show the end of the piece.

Kathy Moody-Arndt, 56
United Methodist Minister

From Barberton, Ohio, Kathy plays piano and keyboard and is interested in singing. Music has become an important part of both her ministry and her marriage. She has a background in classical piano and is just now learning to play rock, blues and jazz. Of her music theory studies, Kathy says, "Theory helps you to understand the music you hear around you. Knowing the theory behind what you hear gives you a new appreciation for it, and a deeper respect for the musicians."

Chapter Five

lesson 5: meter

Vocabulary this page:
meter/simple quadruple/strong beats/
weak beats/simple triple/

The most obvious difference between $\frac{4}{4}$ and $\frac{3}{4}$ is the number of beats per measure; $\frac{3}{4}$ has one less beat than $\frac{4}{4}$. The other difference is a matter of *meter*.

$\frac{4}{4}$ is in *simple quadruple* meter. This means that there are four beats per measure with *strong beats* (more stress) on 1 and 3, 1 being slightly stronger than 3. Beats 2 and 4 are *weak beats*. The word "simple" means that each beat can be divided in two parts (eighth notes).

Here is a melody from Ludwig van Beethoven's *9th Symphony*. Listen to it on the CD or play it on your instrument and think about beats 1 and 3 having a little more "weight" than beats 2 and 4.

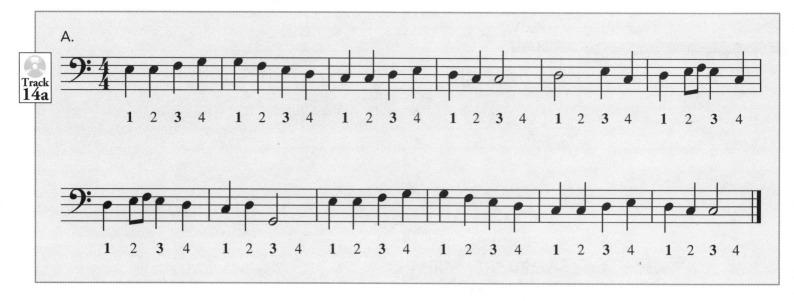

$\frac{3}{4}$ is in *simple triple* meter. This means that there are three beats per measure with the strong beat on beat 1. Here is a portion of the melody from "Scarborough Fair." Listen to it or play it and think of beat 1 as having the most "weight" in each measure.

Beginning Theory for Adults

Chapter Six

lesson 1: keys and key signatures— sharp keys

Vocabulary this page:
key

Keys

On pages 26, you learned about major scales. In certain scales, such as G Major, you put sharps in front of certain notes to make the eight notes of the scale fit the major scale formula:

W–W–H–W–W–W–H

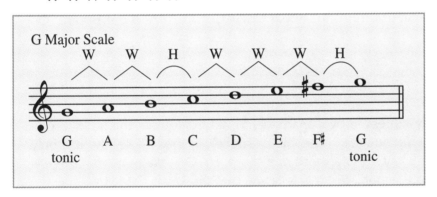

The notes of a major scale comprise the *key* of that scale. For example, on page 26 you learned that a G Major scale is comprised of these notes: G A B C D E F♯ G.

These notes, together, make up the key of G Major. If you compose a piece of music using these notes, particularly if you start and end on the tonic or key note, G, you are writing in the key of G Major.

Vocabulary this page:
key signature

Key Signatures

To make music easier to read and write, all of the accidentals used in a major scale, or a piece in that key, are put together at the beginning of each line of music. This is called the *key signature*. The sharp sign goes on the line or space of the note that is to be sharped. This way, a quick glance at the beginning of a line of music tells you which key you are in and what notes to play sharp or flat.

With a key signature, the G Major scale looks like this:

IMPORTANT NOTE No. 1:
Sharps in a key signature always occur in a specific order: F♯, C♯, G♯, D♯, A♯, E♯ and B♯. To remember this order, you can use this phrase: **F**at **C**ows **G**o **D**own **A**nd **E**at **B**read. Or, make up one of your own.

IMPORTANT NOTE No. 2:
To figure out the key being expressed by a sharp key signature, look at the last sharp in the key signature and think up one step (one line or space). For example, there is only one sharp in G Major, so the key signature has one sharp, F♯. One step up from there is the G space, directly above the staff. So, this tells you that the key is G Major.

On page 28, you used the major scale formula to create an A Major scale. The result was three sharps: F♯, C♯ and G♯. Since G♯ is the last sharp in the key signature, we can think up one step from there to figure out that the key is A Major.

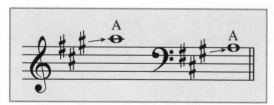

lesson 2: keys and key signatures— flat keys

On page 26, you used a flat to create an F Major scale. On page 28, you also used flats to create the E♭ and A♭ Major scales. These accidentals are also put together in key signatures to simplify reading and writing music.

Here is the E♭ Major scale:

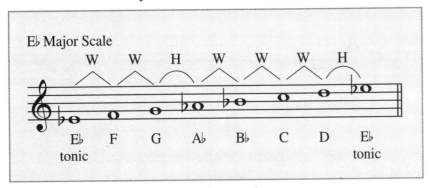

These notes comprise the key of E♭ Major.

Using a key signature, the E♭ Major scale looks like this:

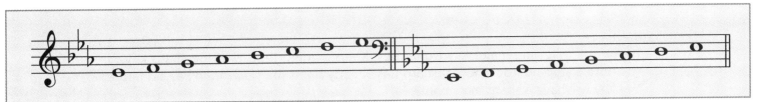

VERY IMPORTANT NOTE No. 3
Flats in a key signature always occur in a specific order: B♭, E♭, A♭, D♭, G♭, C♭ and F♭. To remember this order, you can use this phrase: **Be Ever Alert During Guitar Class, Friend.** Or, make up one of your own.

IMPORTANT NOTE No. 4:
To figure out the key being expressed by a flat key signature, look at the next to last flat in the key signature. That is the key. For example, there are three flats in the E♭ Major scale: B♭, E♭ and A♭. The next to last flat is E♭, so that is the key. The only exception to this is the key of F, which has only one flat in the key signature.

Ear Training Exercises

1. In each of these correctly written major scales, one note will be played incorrectly on the CD. Circle that one.

Track 15

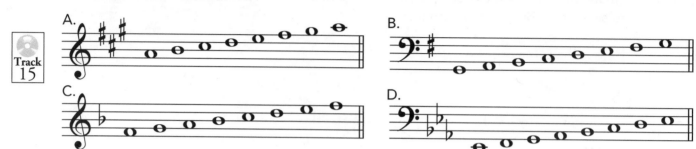

2. Listen to the examples of steps on the CD, and indicate whether they are whole steps or half steps. Use "W" for whole step and "H" for half step.

A. _____ B. _____ C. _____ D. _____ E. _____ F. _____ G. _____ H. _____

Written

3. Name the following major key signatures. Keep in mind that, with the sharp keys, if the note a step up from the last sharp has already been sharped in the key signature, the key will have a sharp in its name.

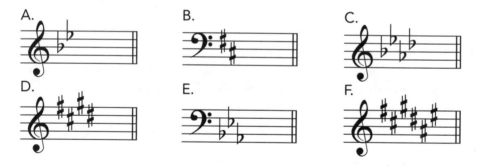

4. Write key signatures for the following keys.

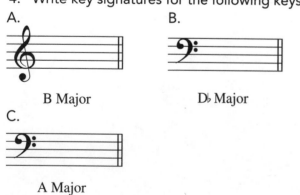

A. B Major

B. D♭ Major

C. A Major

Beginning Theory for Adults

lesson 3: all of the sharp and flat keys

Including the C Major scale, which has no sharps or flats, there are 15 different major scales. There are, however, only 12 different sounding scales, because some of them are enharmonically equivalent (page 25). B Major sounds the same as C♭ Major; F♯ Major sounds the same as G♭ Major; and C♯ Major sounds the same as D♭ Major. Remember, a key signature remains in force until it is changed.

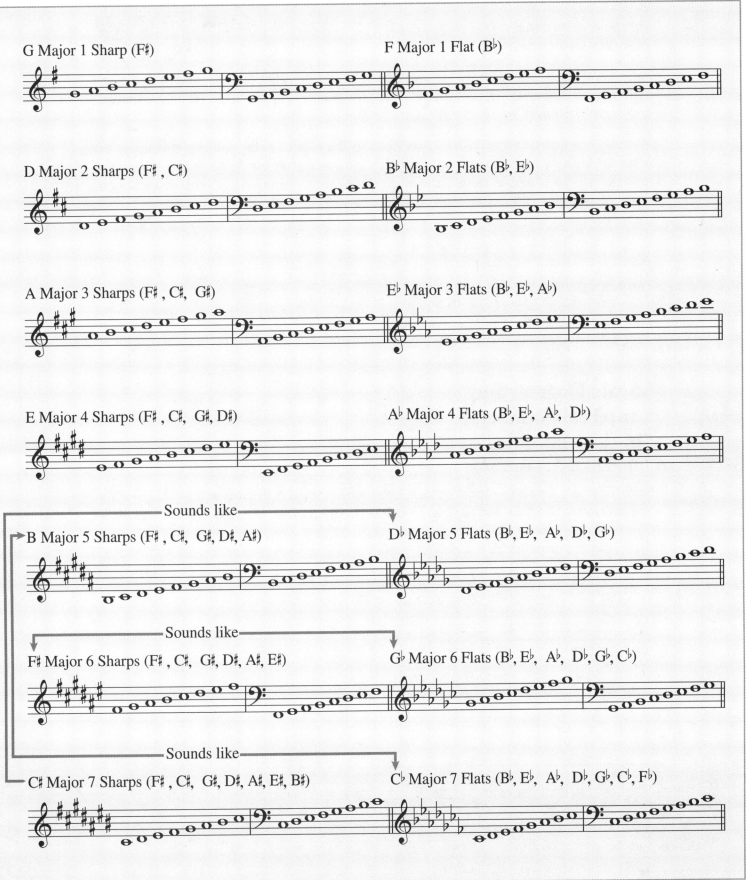

Chapter Seven

lesson 1: introducing intervals

Vocabulary this page:
interval/scale degree

An *interval* is the distance between two notes. You already know three intervals: the half step (page 19), the whole step (page 19) and the octave (page 24). When we think of an interval, however, we ordinarily think of a number.

Intervals are measured from the lower note to the higher note, and the measurement is based on how many steps away in the musical alphabet the higher note is from the lower one. For example, here is the musical alphabet starting on A, with every step of the alphabet given a number showing how many steps they are from the A.

A	B	C	D	E	F	G	A
1	2	3	4	5	6	7	8

The interval from A to B is called a 2nd; the interval from A to C is a 3rd; from A to D is a 4th, etc. The distance from the low A to another low A is called a unison. The distance from the low A to the high A, as you know, is called an octave.

Scale Degrees and Interval Numbers in the Major Scale

Since the major scale is so important to us, let's look at the interval numbers in a C Major scale. The interval numbers are also referred to as scale degrees. They are used as identifiers of the different notes in any major scale. For example, the D is the 2nd scale degree in a C Major scale. On the other hand, it is also an interval of a 2nd from the tonic.

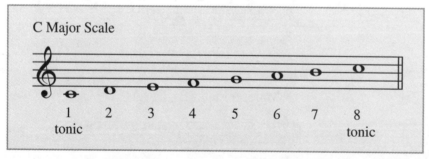

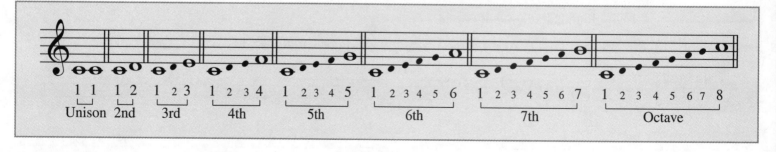

lesson 2: identifying the size of an interval within the major scale

It's easy to look at an interval and quickly deduce its number.

Even numbered intervals (2nds, 4ths, 6ths and octaves) are written from line to space or space to line.

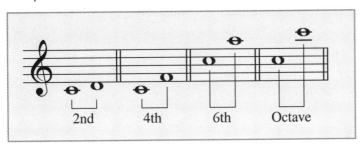

Odd numbered intervals (unison, 3rd, 5ths and 7ths) are written line to line or space to space.

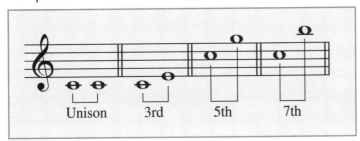

 Exercises

1. Are these even or odd intervals? Circle the correct answers below the staff.

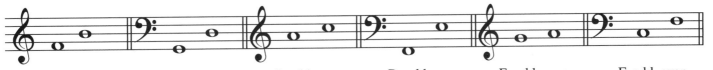

A. odd even   B. odd even   C. odd even   D. odd even   E. odd even   F. odd even

2. On the lines below the staff, name the intervals. For now, always assume that the lower note is the tonic of a major scale. Accidentals do not change the number of the interval.

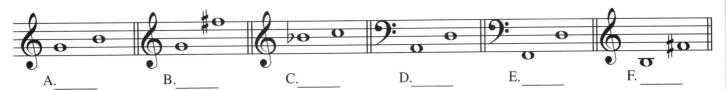

A._____   B._____   C._____   D._____   E._____   F._____

3. Write the interval indicated above these notes.

A. 2nd   B. 3rd   C. 6th   D. 4th   E. 7th   F. 5th

Chapter Seven

lesson 3: melodic vs. harmonic intervals

Vocabulary this page:
melodic interval/harmonic interval/double stops/diads

The intervals we have looked at so far have been *melodic intervals*. A melodic interval is one in which the two notes are sounded one after another.

When the two notes in an interval are sounded together, they are called a *harmonic interval*. When two notes are to be sounded together, they are written one directly on top of the other.

Harmonic intervals are sometimes called *double stops* (this is a term used by string instrument players, such as violinists, for playing two notes at once). This kind of interval can also be called a diad.

Exercises

1. Indicate whether the following intervals are harmonic (Harm.) or melodic (Mel.) by circling the correct answer below the staff. Also indicate the interval's number name.

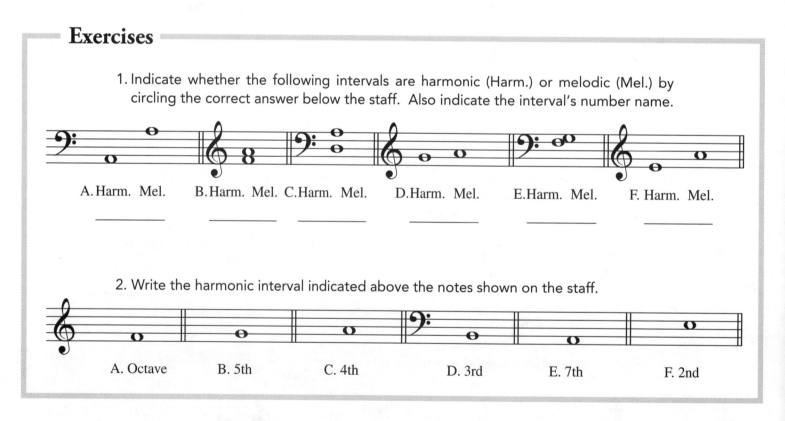

A. Harm. Mel.   B. Harm. Mel.   C. Harm. Mel.   D. Harm. Mel.   E. Harm. Mel.   F. Harm. Mel.

_____   _____   _____   _____   _____   _____

2. Write the harmonic interval indicated above the notes shown on the staff.

A. Octave   B. 5th   C. 4th   D. 3rd   E. 7th   F. 2nd

lesson 4: interval qualities— major and perfect

Vocabulary this page:
quality/associative repertoire

So far, we have been dealing with the number names (including octave and unison) of intervals. Every interval also has a quality name. The quality tells us the characteristic of the interval.

This is where the language of music theory becomes somewhat subjective; you are going to have to learn what words like "major," "minor" and "perfect" mean in terms of aural characteristics. This is not always easy to describe, so the CD that accompanies this book will become invaluable as you continue. Music is, after all, an art, although books such as these can make it seem like a "science" at times. Fortunately, many aspects of music are experienced very similarly by millions of people, which makes discussion possible.

When we measure every scale degree of a major scale against the tonic, we find two kinds of intervals: major and perfect.

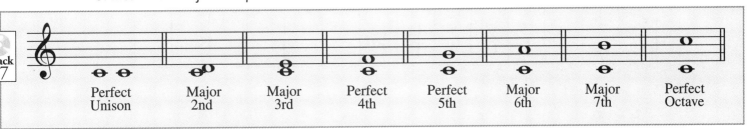

Track 17							
Perfect Unison	Major 2nd	Major 3rd	Perfect 4th	Perfect 5th	Major 6th	Major 7th	Perfect Octave

We think of major intervals as sounding "bright" and "happy." Perfect intervals are more "open-" or "hollow-" sounding.

The more "handles" you have on a concept, the easier it is to grasp. For intervals, we can start with three very important handles:

Three Handles for Grasping Intervals

1. The number of alphabetical steps from the lower note to the upper note, as discussed on pages 40–42

2. The exact distance in half steps between the two notes.

3. The sound—the interval reminds you of a tune that you know which uses that interval.

lesson 5: major and perfect intervals in half steps

Second on the list of three handles for grasping intervals gives us a ruler with which to measure interval distances. A major 2nd, for example, is two half steps from the tonic. A major 3rd is four half steps from the tonic. This handy chart shows how easy it is to measure intervals by counting half steps on a keyboard.

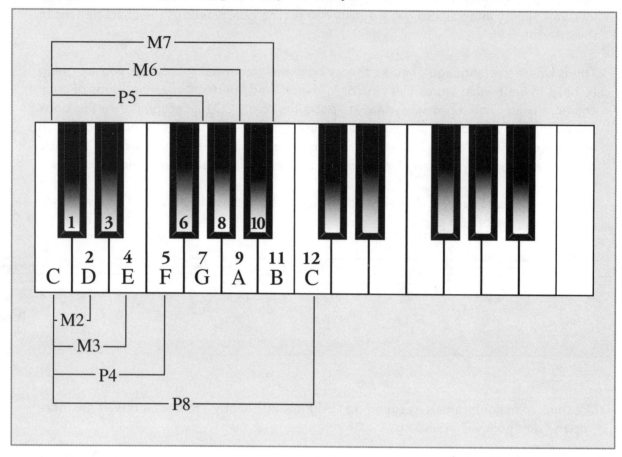

Interval	Abbreviation	No. of Half steps
Perfect Unison	PU	0
Major 2nd	M2	2
Major 3rd	M3	4
Perfect 4th	P4	5
Perfect 5th	P5	7
Major 6th	M6	9
Major 7th	M7	11
Perfect Octave	P8	12

Beginning Theory for Adults

lesson 6: major and perfect intervals associative repertoire

Third on the list of handles for grasping intervals is often called associative repertoire. We associate the sound of the interval with the sound of a familiar song.

Play a major 2nd on your instrument. Then think of the first two notes of "Strangers in the Night" or the vocal melody of "Stairway to Heaven."

Play a major 3rd on your instrument. These are the first two notes of "Michael Row Your Boat Ashore" and "Kum-Ba-Ya."

Play a perfect 4th. It's "Here Comes the Bride!"

Play a perfect 5th. These are the first two notes of "Twinkle, Twinkle, Little Star."

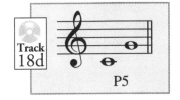

Play a major 6th. These are the first two notes of "My Bonnie Lies Over the Ocean" and "It Came Upon a Midnight Clear."

Play a major 7th. This is where most theory teachers throw up their hands. But, let's take a stab at it. Think of the first and third notes of "Bali Ha'i" from the Rodgers and Hammerstein musical, *South Pacific.* Come on now, this is a book for adults. Somebody reading this must know this tune!

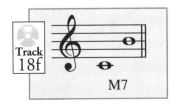

Play a perfect octave. Think of the melody sung on the words "Somewhere, over the rainbow," from *The Wizard of Oz.* The first two notes form a perfect octave.

Ear Training Exercises—Major and Perfect Intervals

 Track 19a DEMONSTRATION. The CD will demonstrate how you can listen to the major scale in your mental musical ear and pick out a major or perfect interval. This is a good strategy for learning to hear these intervals. Also, it is a good idea to review the interval demonstrations on page 43.

 Track 19b 1. Listen to these six melodic intervals. They will either be major 2nds or perfect 5ths. Circle the correct answer.

A. M2 P5   B. M2 P5   C. M2 P5   D. M2 P5   E. M2 P5   F. M2 P5

 Track 20 2. Listen to these six melodic intervals. They will either be major 3rds or major 7ths. Circle the correct answer.

A. M3 M7   B. M3 M7   C. M3 M7   D. M3 M7   E. M3 M7   F. M3 M7

 Track 21 3. Listen to these six melodic intervals. They will either be perfect 4ths or major 7ths. Circle the correct answer.

A. P4 M7   B. P4 M7   C. P4 M7   D. P4 M7   E. P4 M7   F. P4 M7

 Track 22 4. Listen to these six melodic intervals. They will either be perfect octaves or major 6ths. Circle the correct answer.

A. P8 M6   B. P8 M6   C. P8 M6   D. P8 M6   E. P8 M6   F. P8 M6

 Track 23 5. Listen to these six melodic intervals. They will either be major 2nds or major 3rds. Circle the correct answer.

A. M2 M3   B. M2 M3   C. M2 M3   D. M2 M3   E. M2 M3   F. M2 M3

 Track 24 6. Listen to these six melodic intervals. They will either be major 6ths or major 7ths. Circle the correct answer.

A. M6 M7   B. M6 M7   C. M6 M7   D. M6 M7   E. M6 M7   F. M6 M7

 Track 25 7. Listen to the following eight melodic intervals. The lower notes are all C. Using the mental strategy demonstrated in track 19A at the top of the page, determine the interval, and write the correct note above the C. Write the interval number and quality on the line below the staff.

A.   B.   C.   D.   E.   F.   G.   H.

lesson 7: harmonic major and perfect intervals— consonance and dissonance

Vocabulary this page:
consonance/dissonance

As you learned on page 42, when two notes in an interval are played together, it is called a harmonic interval. With harmonic intervals, we have a fourth, very important "handle" for grasping their sounds: whether they are consonant or dissonant. These terms refer to the effect of combinations of pitches.

Consonance means the combined pitches are harmonious, causing a feeling of rest. As you will hear, there are different degrees or types of consonance—from fairly hollow and characterless to rich and sweet. But there is no real tension in consonant intervals; they don't feel like they need to "go" anywhere. Among perfect and major intervals, the consonant intervals are:

1. Perfect Unison

PU

2. Perfect Octave

P8

3. Perfect 5th

P5

4. Major 6th

M6

5. Major 3rd

M3

6. Perfect 4th

P4

The above list progresses from most consonant to least consonant. In some circumstances the perfect 4th can be considered slightly dissonant. Generally, 3rds and 6ths are the considered the "sweetest" intervals. Listen to each interval and think about its quality.

Dissonance means the combined pitches are discordant or have a clashing sound. They create a feeling of tension and unease. There are greater and lesser degrees of dissonance. Among major and perfect intervals, the dissonant intervals are:

1. Major 2nd
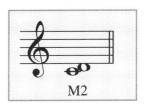
M2

2. Major 7th

M7

Because the upper note of a major 7th interval is so close to the octave of the tonic, it is generally considered to be the more dissonant of the two intervals. Listen to them both and think about their qualities.

Chapter Seven

Exercises—Major and Perfect Intervals

1. Identify these intervals. Write the number of half steps on the lines below the staff. Write the quality and number names on the lines above the staff.

Interval:

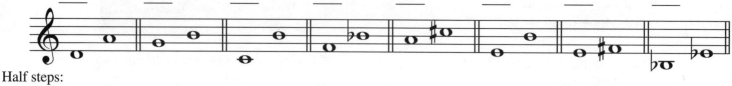

Half steps:

Interval:

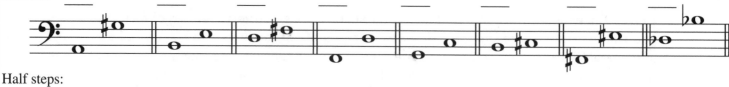

Half steps:

2. Write harmonic intervals above these notes as indicated under the staff.

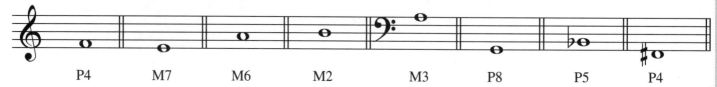

P4   M7   M6   M2   M3   P8   P5   P4

3. Listen to this example in G Major. Draw the missing notes and rhythms in the boxes provided.

4. Listen to the harmonic intervals played on the notes shown below on the CD. Identify each interval (use abbreviations) and draw the top note on the staff. First, ask yourself if it is consonant or dissonant. Then, how consonant or how dissonant is it? Also, are the notes close together or further apart? Answering these questions will help you identify the intervals. Review the CD track on page 45, first. Each interval will be played twice. Have fun!

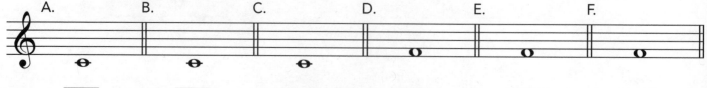

Beginning Theory for Adults

lesson 8: the circle of 5ths

Vocabulary this page:
Circle of 5ths/cycle of 5ths/circle or cycle of 4ths

You can use your knowledge of intervals to enhance your understanding of key signatures. Look at the diagram of the *circle of 5ths* (often called the *cycle of 5ths*). If you progress clockwise around the circle, it shows how the keys relate to one another by the number of sharps and flats in the key signature, and the order in which the sharps and flats occur.

It's important to know that in jazz and blues, this is often viewed counter clockwise rather than clockwise, and thought of as a *circle (or cycle) of 4ths*.

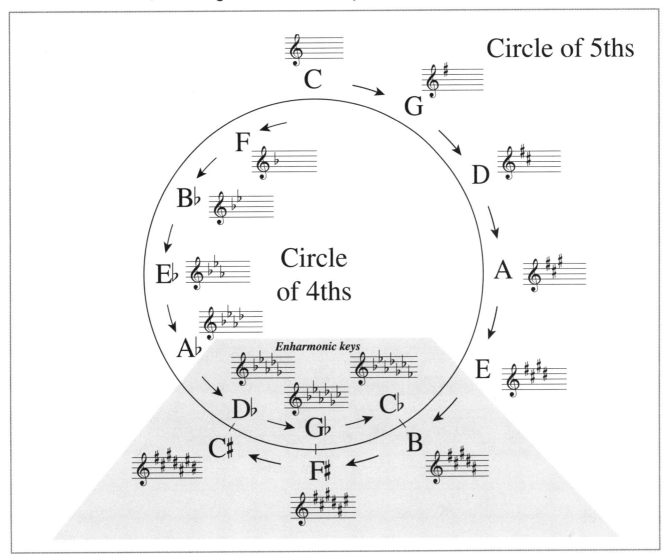

When going clockwise, which is up by perfect 5ths, one new sharp is added to each new key. If you play the first five notes of a major scale in a key, the fifth note, which is a perfect 5th from the tonic, becomes the tonic of the new key.

When going counter clockwise, which is up by perfect 4ths, one new flat is added to each new key. If you play the first four notes of a major scale, the fourth note, which is a perfect 4th from the tonic, becomes the tonic of a new key.

Remember: The order of sharps in the key signature is F C G D A E B. The order of flats in the key signature is B E A D G C F.

lesson 9: minor intervals

Vocabulary this page:
minor interval

A *minor interval* is one half step smaller than the major interval with the same number name. For example, the interval of a major 3rd is four half steps, so a minor 3rd is three half steps.

You can change a major interval (M) to a minor interval (m) by lowering the top note one half step.

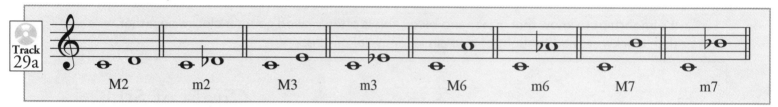

Or, you can raise the lower interval one half step.

The following minor intervals occur within a one-octave major scale between the following scale degrees:

Minor 2nd: from 3 to 4, 7 to 8
Minor 3rd: from 2 to 4, 3 to 5, 6 to 8
Minor 6th: from 3 to 8
Minor 7th: 2 to 8

Minor Intervals Within a One-Octave Major Scale

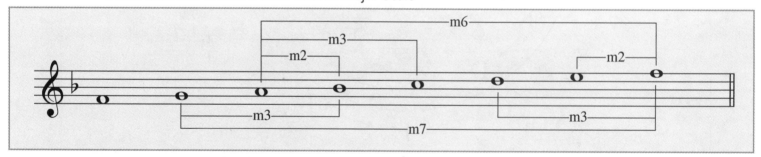

Exercises

1. Change these major intervals to minor intervals by lowering the top note with an accidental. Draw the new interval and label it below.

M3 _____   M6 _____   M7 _____   M2 _____

2. Change these major intervals to minor intervals by raising the lower note using an accidental. Draw the new interval and label it below.

M6 _____   M2 _____   M3 _____   M7 _____

Beginning Theory for Adults

lesson 10: double sharps and double flats

Vocabulary this page:
double sharp/double flat

✖ A *double sharp* raises the pitch of a note by two half steps (one whole step). Use this sign to raise the pitch of a note that is already sharp. On the keyboard, this is two keys above the natural note.

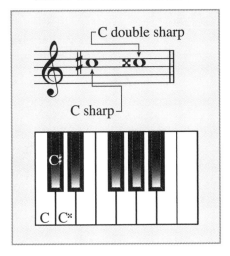

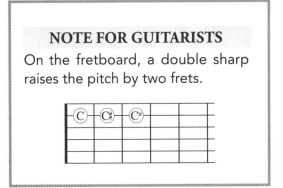

NOTE FOR GUITARISTS

On the fretboard, a double sharp raises the pitch by two frets.

𝄫 A *double flat* lowers the pitch of a note by two half steps (one whole step). Use this sign to lower the pitch of a note that is already flat. On the keyboard, this is two keys below the natural note.

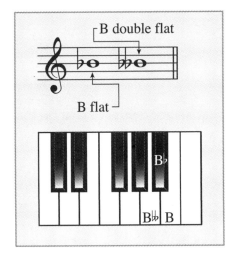

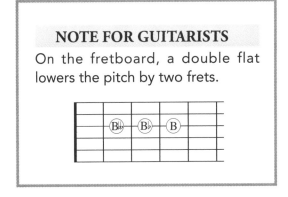

NOTE FOR GUITARISTS

On the fretboard, a double flat lowers the pitch by two frets.

lesson 11: augmented and diminished intervals

Vocabulary this page:
augment/diminish

To augment something is to make it bigger. When the notes of a major or perfect interval are made one half step further apart—when the interval is increased by one half step—it becomes an augmented interval. This can be done by raising the upper note or lowering the lower note.

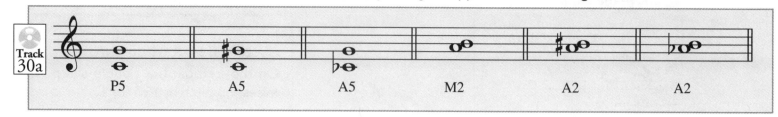

To diminish something is to make it smaller. When the notes of a perfect interval are made one half step closer together—when the interval is decreased by one half step—it becomes a diminished interval. This can be done by lowering the upper note or raising the lower note. (Remember, major intervals become minor when made smaller.)

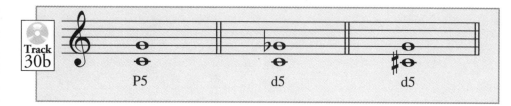

The intervals of an augmented 5th, augmented 6th and augmented 2nd are enharmonically equivalent to the minor 6th, minor 7th and minor 3rd, respectively.

Exercises

1. Make these major and perfect intervals augmented using an accidental to change the top note. Draw the new interval and label it below.

P5 _____   M6 _____   M2 _____   P4 _____

2. Make these perfect intervals diminished using an accidental to change the top note. Draw the new interval and label it below.

P5 _____   P5 _____   P5 _____   P5 _____

Beginning Theory for Adults

lesson 12: learning to identify minor, diminished and augmented intervals

Here is a chart like the one on page 44, but this time it includes the minor, diminished and augmented intervals.

Interval	Abbreviation	Number of Half steps	
Perfect Unison	PU	0	
Minor 2nd	m2	1	
Major 2nd	M2	2	
Augmented 2nd	A2	3	enharmonically equivalent
Minor 3rd	m3	3	
Major 3rd	M3	4	
Perfect 4th	P4	5	
Augmented 4th	A4	6	enharmonically equivalent
Diminished 5th	d5	6	
Perfect 5th	P5	7	
Augmented 5th	A5	8	enharmonically equivalent
Minor 6th	m6	8	
Major 6th	M6	9	
Augmented 6th	A6	10	enharmonically equivalent
Minor 7th	m7	10	
Major 7th	M7	11	
Perfect 0ctave	P8	12	

You may have noticed that certain intervals were omitted from the list: augmented unison, augmented 3rd, diminished 4th, augmented 7th and diminished octave. These intervals are rarely, if ever, used. Almost always, the enharmonic equivalent is more logical and practical.

Exercises

1. Identify these minor, augmented or diminished intervals by writing the sizes in half steps on the lines below the staff and the interval quality and number names on the lines above the staff (use abbreviations). Remember, odd numbered intervals are written line to line or space to space. Even numbered intervals are written space to line or line to space (page 41).

lesson 13: minor, diminished and augmented melodic intervals associative repertoire

Play a minor 2nd on your instrument. These are the first two notes of the "Für Elise" by Beethoven and the theme from the movie, *The Pink Panther*. They are also the first two notes of the song "A Hard Day's Night" by the Beatles and the song "Till There was You."

Play an augmented 2nd or minor 3rd (they are enharmonic equivalents). These are the first two notes of "Greensleeves (What Child is This?)" and "This Old Man." These are also the first two notes of "Georgia on My Mind" and the opening riff of "Smoke on the Water."

Play an augmented 4th or diminished 5th (they are enharmonic equivalents). These are the first two notes of "Maria" from *West Side Story* by Leonard Bernstein.

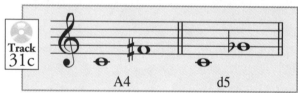

Play an augmented 5th or minor 6th (they are enharmonic equivalents). These are the first two notes of "Equinox" by John Coltrane and "Where Do I Begin," the theme to the movie, *Love Story*.

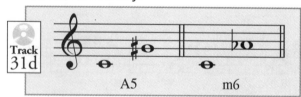

Play an augmented 6th or minor 7th (they are enharmonic equivalents). These are the first two notes of "Somewhere (There's a Place for Us)" from *West Side Story* by Leonard Bernstein.

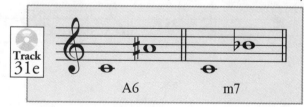

lesson 14: minor, diminished and augmented harmonic intervals

Vocabulary this page:
tritone

As with major and perfect intervals, harmonic minor, diminished and augmented intervals range from very consonant to very dissonant. The consonant intervals are:

Minor 3rd (augmented 2nd)

Minor 6th (augmented 5th)

Among minor, diminished and augmented intervals, there are more dissonant intervals:

Minor 7th (augmented 6th)

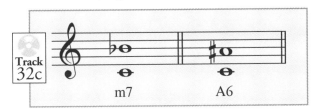

Minor 2nd

Augmented 4th (Diminished 5th, tritone)
Since the size of this interval is three whole steps (six half steps), it is often called a *tritone*. It is considered one of the most dissonant intervals.

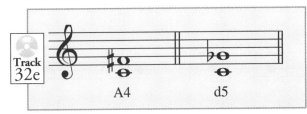

Chapter Seven

Chapter Eight

lesson 1: dotted quarter notes and rests

On page 32, you learned that when a dot is added to the right of a note, its value is increased by one half. Because of this, a dotted half note has a value of three beats. By the same token, a dotted quarter note has a value of one and a half beats. It is like a quarter note tied to an eighth note.

The same is true for a dotted quarter rest; it will have a value of one and a half beats of silence.

It is quite common to find a dotted quarter note combined with an eighth note to create a long-short rhythm. It is helpful to subdivide the beats by eighth notes when counting this rhythm. This makes it very clear that a dotted quarter value is equal to three eighth notes.

Exercises

1. To the right of the equal sign, write the sum of the values of the notes that are to the left of the equal sign.

2. Circle the measure that has too many beats.

lesson 2: major triads

Vocabulary this page:
chord/accompany/harmony/triad/root/
3rd/5th/chord symbol/root position

When three or more notes are played together, they form a *chord*. Chords are often used to *accompany* (provide a background for) melodies. The study of chords and how they relate to each other and to melodies is called the study of *harmony*. The chords in a piece are often called "the harmony."

The most basic kind of chord is called a *triad* and has three notes called the *root*, *3rd* and *5th*. The notes of a triad can be derived from a scale or created by stacking the intervals of a 3rd and a 5th above the bottom note, which is called the *root*. The root is the note that gives the chord its name. For example, when a chord is built above the note C, the C is the root and the chord is a C chord.

Just as intervals have various qualities with specific characteristics, so too each chord has a specific quality with specific characteristics. The *major triad* can be made by combining the tonic (1st), 3rd and 5th degrees of a major scale built on the root. For example, a C Major triad uses C (the tonic of a C Major scale), E (the third scale degree) and G (the fifth scale degree).

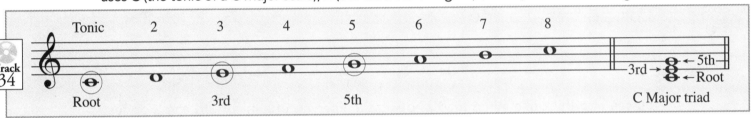

You can also think of a major triad as being the intervals of a major 3rd and a perfect 5th stacked above the root. Also, notice that the intervals from the 3rd to the 5th is a minor 3rd. These are the characteristics that make a triad major.

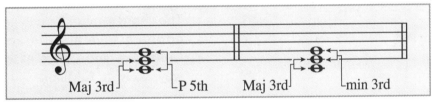

A triad with the root on the bottom is said to be in root position. The three notes of a triad always include every other note letter name in the musical alphabet (A–C–E, B–D–F, C–E–G, D–F–A, and so on) starting from the root. The three notes, when written in root position, are always all on spaces or all on lines. You can build a triad on any note of any scale.

CHORD SYMBOLS

In pop, jazz, blues and rock music, *chord symbols* appear above the staff to show what chord to play. The chord symbol for a major chord is most often just the name of the root. For example, a C Major chord symbol would simply be "C."

Exercises

1. Draw notes to form triads above these notes.

2. Draw notes to create major triads above these notes. Use accidentals where necessary.

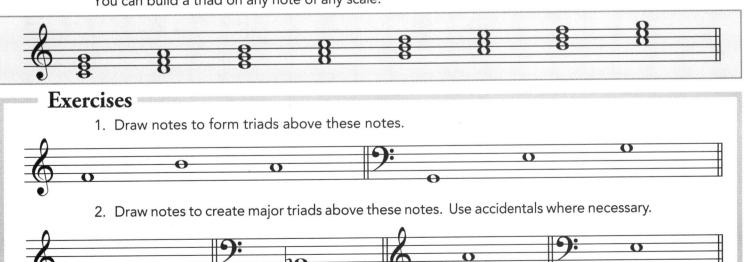

lesson 3: minor triads

Vocabulary this page:
♭3rd

A minor triad can be created by lowering the 3rd of a major triad one half step. A C Major triad is C-E-G, so a minor triad is C-E♭-G. You can use the same process as you did with the major triad to derive the triad from the major scale, with the additional step of lowering the 3rd.

In "jazz theory," which includes any theory discussion pertaining to jazz, blues, rock and other forms of popular music, it is commonplace to relate chords and scales to the major scale. A flat is used to indicate a note one half step lower than its position in the major scale, even if the note does not have a flat. For example, the 3rd of an A Major scale is C-sharp and the "♭3rd" is C natural. Likewise, sharps are used to indicate that a note is one half step higher than its position in the major scale.

Here is the minor triad as derived from the major scale:

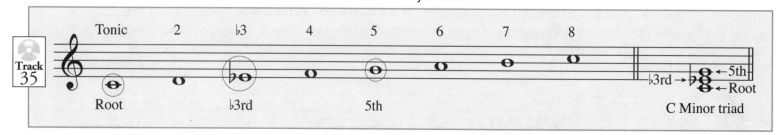

You can also think of a minor triad as being the intervals of a minor 3rd and a perfect 5th stacked above the root. Also, notice that the intervals from the ♭3rd to the 5th is a major 3rd. These are the characteristics that make a triad minor. This triad is thought of as having a tragic or sad sound.

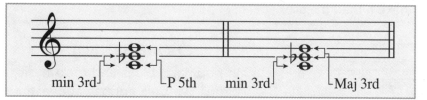

CHORD SYMBOLS

The chord symbol for a minor chord appears several different ways: Cmin, Cm and C- are all common ways to write C Minor.

Exercises

1. Change these major triads into minor triads by changing the 3rds. Use or change accidentals as necessary.

2. Draw notes and use accidentals as necessary to create minor triads above these roots. Label each one above the staff.

3. You will hear six triads (A–F). Which are major and which are minor? Circle your answers.

    A. Major Minor   B. Major Minor   C. Major Minor

    D. Major Minor   E. Major Minor   F. Major Minor

lesson 4: diminished triads

A diminished triad can be created by lowering the 3rd and 5th of a major triad one half step, or by lowering the 5th of a minor triad. A C Major triad is C-E-G, so a diminished triad is C-E♭-G♭. You can use the same process as you did with the major triad to derive the triad from the major scale, with the additional steps of lowering the 3rd and the 5th.

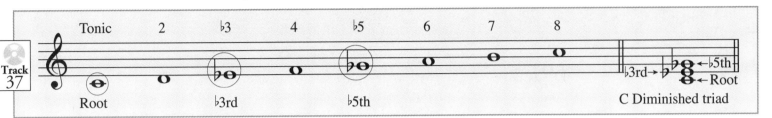

You can also think of a diminished triad as being the intervals of a minor 3rd and a diminished 5th (tritone) stacked above the root. Also, notice that the intervals from the ♭3rd to the ♭5th is a minor 3rd—we have stacked two minor 3rds. These are the characteristics that make a triad diminished. This triad is thought of as having a sinister sound, probably due to the dissonance of the diminished 5th.

CHORD SYMBOL

The chord symbol for a diminished triad is often written like this: C°. It also appears as Cdim.

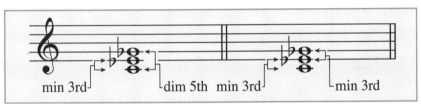

Exercises

In the exercises below, it is helpful to remember double flats and double sharps.

1. Change these major triads into diminished triads by changing the 3rds and 5ths.

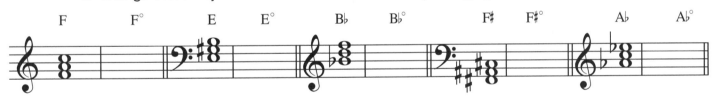

2. Change these minor triads into diminished triads by changing the 5ths.

3. Draw diminished triads above these roots. Use accidentals as necessary.

4. Are these major, minor or diminished triads (are they happy-, sad- or sinister-sounding?). Circle your answers.

A. Major Minor Diminished   B. Major Minor Diminished   C. Major Minor Diminished

D. Major Minor Diminished   E. Major Minor Diminished   F. Major Minor Diminished

lesson 5: augmented triads

An augmented triad can be created by raising the 3rd and 5th of a major triad one half step. A C Major triad is C-E-G, so an augmented triad is C-E-G♯. You can use the same process as you did with the major triad to derive the triad from the major scale, with the additional step of raising the 5th.

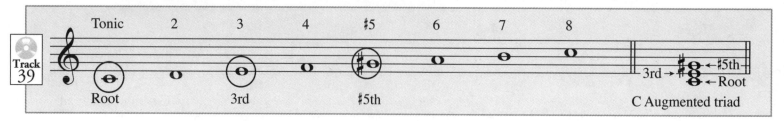

You can also think of an augmented triad as being the intervals of a major 3rd and an augmented 5th stacked above the root. Also, notice that the interval from the 3rd to the ♯5th is a major 3rd—we have stacked two major 3rds. These are the characteristics that make a triad augmented. This triad is thought of as having a strange, ambiguous sound. It is sometimes used to create an atmosphere of tense expectancy or anticipation.

CHORD SYMBOLS

The chord symbol for an augmented triad is often written like this: C+. It also appears as Caug.

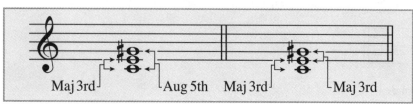

Exercises

Again, don't forget about double sharps and double flats!

1. Change these major triads into augmented triads by changing the 5th.

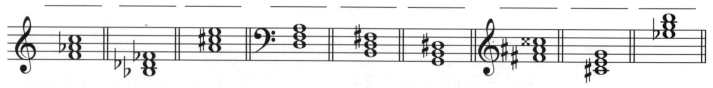

2. Identify these triads. Are they major, minor, diminished or augmented? Write the appropriate chord symbols on the lines above.

3. You will hear six triads. Identify their qualities: major, minor, diminished or augmented. Circle your answers. You'll hear each triad several times.

A. Major	Minor	Diminished	Augmented
B. Major	Minor	Diminished	Augmented
C. Major	Minor	Diminished	Augmented
D. Major	Minor	Diminished	Augmented
E. Major	Minor	Diminished	Augmented
F. Major	Minor	Diminished	Augmented

NOTE FOR GUITARISTS

Most guitar students learn some chords right at the very beginning of their studies. This is natural, since the guitar is so often used to accompany songs. Guitarists are sometimes confused by initial theory lessons about triads because they rarely play a chord that has only three notes. Except for perhaps a few "easy" versions of guitar chords, beginning guitarists are normally strumming four, five or six strings.

To make the guitar sound as full as possible, especially in cases when it is the only instrument accompanying a song, bigger *voicings* are used. A voicing is the specific arrangement of chord tones (the notes in a chord). Most guitar voicings include doublings. To double a chord tone is to use the same note in two (or more) octaves. The chord may only include the three notes of a triad, but some of the notes are used more than once.

For example, we know that a C Major triad has these three notes: C–E–G. But, as the example below demonstrates, the most common guitar voicing of the chord is as follows (from the bottom up): C–E–G–C–E. Both the root (C) and the 3rd (E) are doubled. Five strings are strummed.

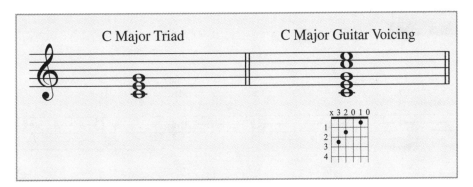

Here is another sample of a triad voiced for the guitar. The chord tones of a G Major triad are: G–B–D. The most common guitar voicing for a G Major triad is as follows: G–B–D–G–B–G. The root (G) is tripled and the 3rd (B) is doubled. Six strings are strummed.

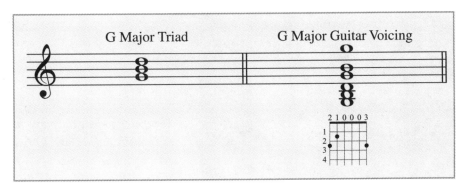

Chapter Eight

lesson 6: diatonic harmony

Vocabulary this page:
diatonic

From the point of view of a music theorist, we are now getting into the really fun stuff. We are going to take a look at what chords exist in a key, and this will lead to discussions of how they relate to each other and how they "behave."

A lot of the music fundamentals you have been learning start to come together now, so make sure you have successfully completed all of the exercises offered thus far. Be sure that you have checked all of your answers against the answer key in the back of the book, and that you understand all the answers.

As you learned on page 57, a triad can be built on every scale degree of the major scale (which you learned all the way back on page 26). You have also learned the four types of triads. Let's take a look at those which occur in a major key. These chords are called the *diatonic harmonies of a major key. Diatonic* means "belonging to the key."

 ## Diatonic Harmonies of the Major Scale

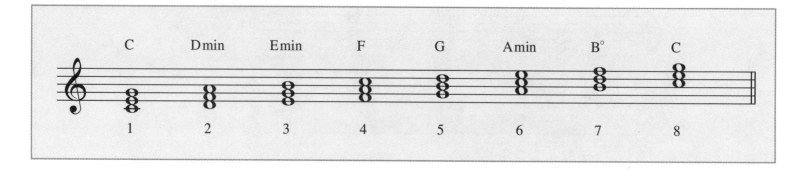

Beth, 33
Portfolio Manager

"Learning to play the piano has been really rewarding! It's fun playing music by some of my favorite artists, such as Tori Amos and Alicia Keyes. It's a pastime that brings both enjoyment and a sense of achievement."

The Primary Chords

As you can easily see by inspecting the chord symbols, three types of triads occur naturally when a triad is built on each note of the major scale: major (on scale degrees 1, 4 and 5), minor (on 2, 3 and 6) and diminished (on 7). In a major key, there are no augmented triads. The three major chords in a major key, built on scale degrees 1, 4 and 5 are called the primary chords. Many songs and compositions are based on the interaction of these three harmonies.

Roman Numerals

Musicians all over the world use a system of labeling chords of a key with Roman numerals. Uppercase Roman numerals are used to label major chords and lowercase Roman numerals used for minor and diminished chords. Diminished chords are also labeled with the same sign used in the chord symbol, ○.

Here's a quick review of Roman numerals:

I .... i 1		V ...... v 5	
II ...... ii 2		VI .... vi 6	
III .... iii 3		VII ... vii 7	
IV .... iv 4			

Here are the diatonic triads again, this time labeled with Roman numerals, and with the three primary chords highlighted.

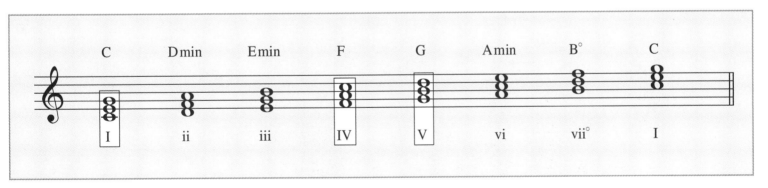

lesson 7: basics of chord function—
the primary chords

Vocabulary this page:
progression

As promised, we will now begin to talk about how chords "behave." One chord on its own doesn't "do" anything. Chords in a *chord progression*, the movement from one chord to the next in a series of chords, will usually follow one of a number of known patterns. Each chord fulfills a function in the pattern. Whether we have studied music or not, as we grow up in our culture, our ears learn to expect these patterns. Recognizing these patterns, and the expectations that arise from this recognition, is what helps us make sense of music. Again, this is a natural process and does not require music training.

The more music training you have, however, the more you will understand what you hear, and the more pleasure you will derive from the little musical surprises the better composers and songwriters provide. You will start to "get" some of the "inside" musical jokes and hear clever nuances in the music you hear every day.

Let's start by the most important chord functions: those of the three primary chords (page 63)—I, IV and V.

Tonic

As you know, the first note in a major scale is called the tonic. This is also the name given to the I chord in a key. The tonic chord is home base for the harmony. Once a chord progression leaves the tonic, it strives to return there, and all of the fun is in the route taken on the journey back to the tonic. Think of the tonic as being stable; it is a resting place for a chord progression.

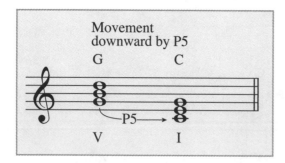

Vocabulary this page:
root movement/dominant/subdominant

Dominant

The chord that is the most likely to lead us to the tonic (I) is the V chord, which we call the dominant. Think of it as being the strongest chord—it has a strong attraction to the tonic. The dominant makes us feel that the music "wants" to go to the tonic. Play this series of chords: C–G–C–G. This is I–V–I–V: tonic-dominant-tonic-dominant. Stopping on the dominant makes us feel like we want to hear one more chord, the tonic. Pay special attention to the fact that the root of the dominant is a perfect 5th above the root of the tonic. This kind of *root movement*, down a perfect 5th, as in V to I, is very important in many chord progressions. Our ears are conditioned to expect this kind of root movement.

Subdominant

While V (dominant) is a perfect 5th above the tonic, IV is a perfect 5th below, which is why it is called the *subdominant*. It is the chord most likely to precede the dominant on the journey back to the tonic. You can think of the chord progression I–IV–V–I as essentially summing up what many chord progressions do.

* It begins on the tonic, I.
* It then moves away to someplace new, IV, the subdominant, which is downward root movement of a 5th.
* It goes to V (dominant), which is the only diatonic harmony that can provide downward root movement of a 5th back to the tonic.
* It returns home to the tonic, I.

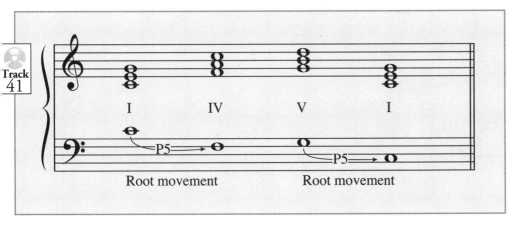

Many popular songs are based on this progression, as are many classical compositions. As you will see, tonic, subdominant and dominant are the three main chord categories. While the other scale degrees have important chords with their own names, functionally, they all fit into one of these three categories, which is why they are called the primary chords.

Exercises

1. Write the appropriate major scale for each key signature given below. Put each scale degree directly above one of the lines shown below the staff. Then, draw a triad over each scale degree and label them with Roman numerals on the lines below the staff. Finally, circle the three primary chords.

A.

B.

C.

D.

2. The following chords are all in the key of A Major. On the lines below the staff, label them with the correct Roman numerals.

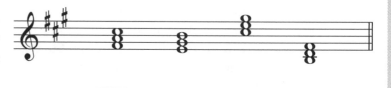

3. Write the three primary chords, I, IV and V, in the keys shown below. Write the names of the keys under the key signatures.

A.

_____   I   IV   V

B.

_____   I   IV   V

C.

_____   I   IV   V

4. The I chord is also called the _____.

5. The IV chord is also called the _____.

6. The V chord is also called the _____.

lesson 8: the three chord categories

Vocabulary this page:
supertonic/mediant/submendiant/leading tone/resolve

Here are all of the chord function names in major diatonic harmony:

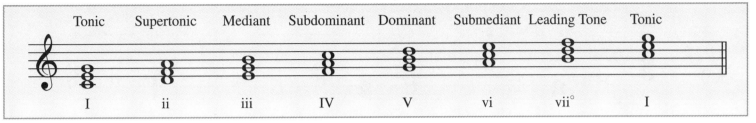

Each of the chords falls into at least one of the three primary chord categories—tonic, subdominant or dominant—because they share notes in common with them.

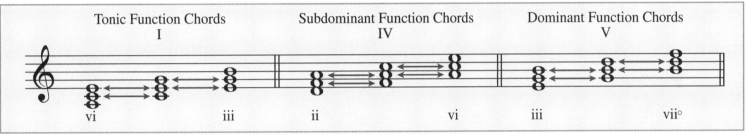

Any chord in a category can act as a substitute for the main chord in the category. The most common example of this is the *supertonic* (ii). In reality, ii is used more than IV in some styles. This is because ii allows downward root movement by 5th to approach V. This makes ii–V–I a powerful progression that uses only downward root movement by 5th.

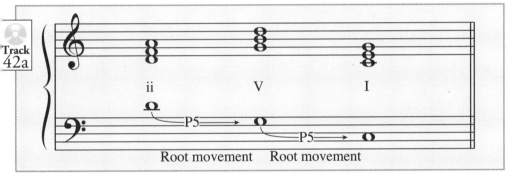

This is overwhelmingly the most important chord progression in jazz and pop music. It is commonly used in other styles of music, too, including classical music of the 18th and 19th centuries.

The leading tone also has an extremely important function, not only as a chord, but also as a note in certain other chords. The leading tone, which is just one half step below the tonic, has a powerful, almost magnetic, attraction to the tonic. Play the old musical ditty, "shave and a haircut, two bits."

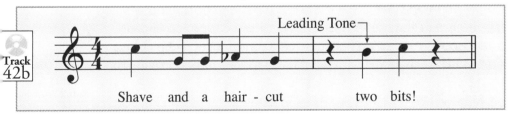

Now try playing it without the last note, stopping on the leading tone. That would keep some people awake at night! That's the power of the leading tone. It needs to resolve to the tonic. To resolve is to release the tension inherent in a melody note or chord by moving to a more stable note or chord. The leading tone, which is the 3rd of the dominant chord, combined with the desireable downward root movement by 5th, makes V to I an extremely satisfying resolution.

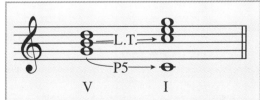

Chapter Eight

Exercises

1. Analyze the chord progressions in the keys shown. Write the name of the key on the line under the key signature. Label each chord with a chord symbol on the lines above the staff, and a Roman numeral on the lines below the staff.

2. You will hear four chord progressions, A through D. Four chord progressions are shown below. Label each chord progression 1, 2, 3 or 4 when you hear it on the CD.

Track 43

No. 1 I–IV–V–I   No. 2 I–ii–V–I   No. 3 I–IV–V–vi   No. 4 I–vi–IV–V

A. _____   B. _____   C. _____   D. _____

3. The ii chord is also called the _____ .

4. The iii chord is also called the _____ .

5. The vi chord is also called the _____ .

6. The vii chord is also called the _____ .

7. The iii and vi chords can both function as _____ .

8. The iii and vii chords can both function as _____ .

9. The ii and vi chords can both function as _____ .

Check the true statements (there can be more than one):

10. A. _____ V to I is a strong progression because the leading tone, which is the 3rd of V, wants to resolve to the tonic.
    B. _____ V to I is a strong progression because the root movement is down by 4th.
    C. _____ V to I is a strong progression because the root movement is down by 5th.

11. A. _____ V to vi is a good progression because vi is a tonic function chord, and dominant function chords such as V want to go to tonic function chords.
    B. _____ V to vi is a not a very good progression because vi is a tonic function chord, and dominant function chords such as V do not want to go to tonic function chords.

12. A. _____ ii should not be followed by V, because the subdominant should precede the dominant in a progression.
    B. _____ ii should be followed by V, because the subdominant should precede the dominant in a progression.

Chapter Nine

lesson 1: the relative minor

Vocabulary this page:
relative minor key/relative minor scale/relative major

As you know, there are 15 different major keys and key signatures (see Chapter 6 starting on page 35). For every major key, there is also a minor key with the same key signature. This is called the relative minor key.

For every major scale, there is a minor scale with exactly the same notes. This is called the relative minor scale. The relative minor scale is built on the 6th degree of a major scale. The 6th degree becomes the tonic (or keynote) of the relative minor scale.

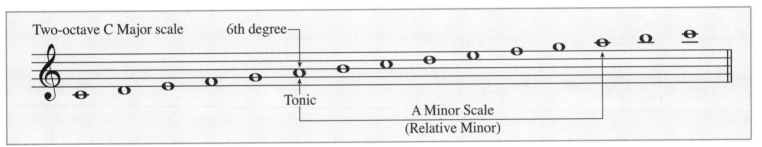

The key of A Minor is the relative minor of C Major. C Major is the relative major key of A Minor.

Another way to find the relative minor of a major key is to think down a minor 3rd from the tonic of the major key. To find the relative major of a minor key, think up a minor 3rd.

Here is a two-octave G Major scale showing the relative minor key. Notice that the same key signature, one sharp (F-sharp), works for both.

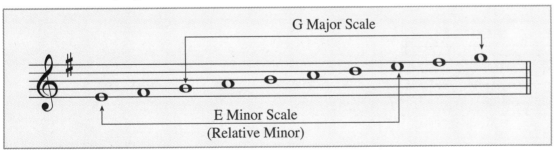

Exercises

Write a two-octave D Major scale (use the correct key signature) and mark the relative minor scale.

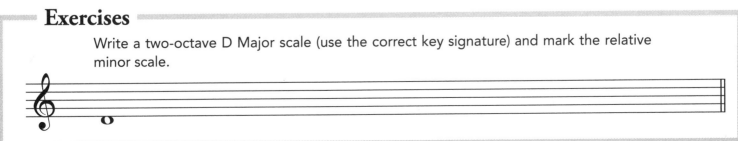

lesson 2: the natural, harmonic and melodic minor scales

Vocabulary this page:
natural minor/parallel major/minor tetrachord

Natural Minor

As you know, the relative minor scale has exactly the same notes as its relative major. Nothing is changed except for the note we start on. For that reason it is called the *natural minor* scale. If you compare a natural minor scale to its *parallel major*—a major scale starting on the same tonic—you will find that the 3rd, 6th and 7th degrees of the minor scale are lowered one half step from their positions in the major scale. Jazz, blues and rock musicians think of these notes in the natural minor scale as ♭3, ♭6, and ♭7, whether they are flat notes or not.

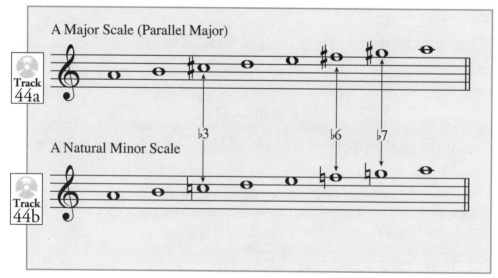

The first four notes of the natural minor scale is a *minor tetrachord*.

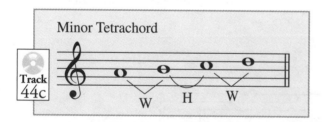

So the natural minor scale formula is 1, 2, ♭3, 4, 5, ♭6, ♭7, 8 (1). It is these lowered notes, particularly the ♭3, which is a minor 3rd above the tonic, that create the sound of the minor scale.

Harmonic Minor

The *harmonic minor* scale does not have a ♭7. Put another way, if we raise the 7th degree of a natural minor scale, we have harmonic minor: 1, 2, ♭3, 4, 5, ♭6, 7, 8 (1). It is the augmented 2nd interval from ♭6 to 7 that creates the exotic sound of the harmonic scale.

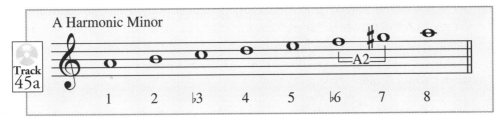

Melodic Minor

The melodic minor scale descends differently than it ascends. Raise both the ♭6 and ♭7 of the natural minor scale to create the ascending melodic scale, and lower them back to their original positions to descend. The descending melodic minor scale is the same as the natural minor scale. The upper tetrachord (page 27) of the ascending melodic minor scale is a major tetrachord. The upper four notes of the descending melodic minor scale is a minor tetrachord.

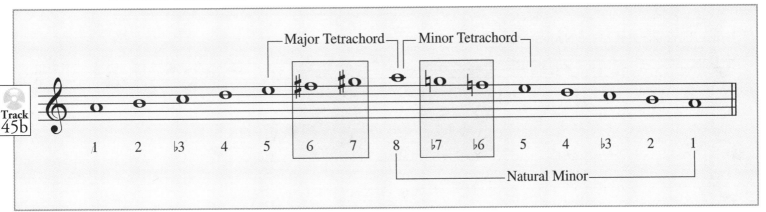

lesson 3: diatonic minor harmony

Vocabulary this page:
jazz minor

The natural minor scale is sometimes called *pure minor*. It represents the minor side of a major key. The melodic minor is the result of the observation that, historically, many classical composers wrote melodies that used a major tetrachord to ascend to the tonic note, even when composing in a minor key. This was probably in order to smoothly approach the tonic note with a leading tone. Remember, the leading tone has a powerful attraction to the tonic.

The harmonic minor scale exists solely to justify a logical collection of minor-sounding harmonies that still includes the powerful dominant harmony (a major chord built on the 5th degree of the scale that includes a leading tone as the 3rd of the chord).

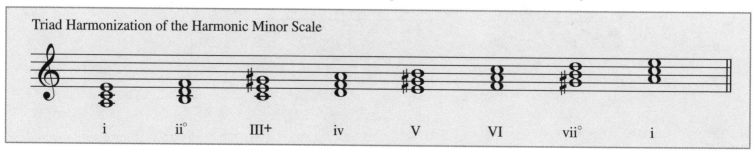

Triad Harmonization of the Harmonic Minor Scale

The important features of minor diatonic harmony are that i is minor, III+ is augmented, V is still major and both ii and vii are diminished. Since there are three versions of the minor scale, there are lots of variations in the harmony to pieces in minor keys. For example, sometimes v is minor, because that is diatonic to the natural minor scale.

Here are the diatonic harmonies in the natural and ascending melodic minor (sometimes called *jazz minor*, since jazz players do not play the descending melodic minor any differently than the ascending part of the scale).

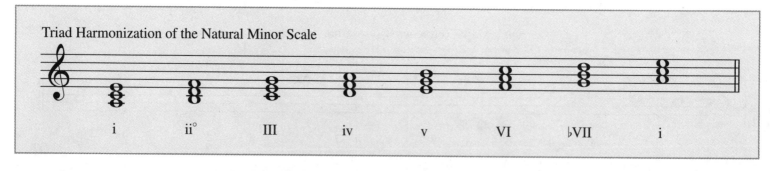

Triad Harmonization of the Natural Minor Scale

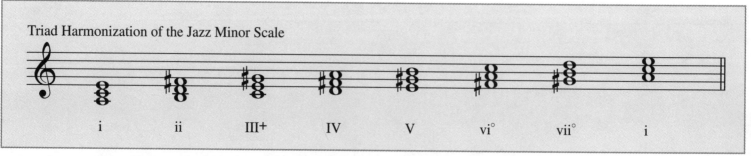

Triad Harmonization of the Jazz Minor Scale

As you can see, there is a rich variety of choices for minor key harmonies.

Exercises

1. Write an F Major scale on the staff below. Use the correct key signature.

2. Write the relative minor scale of F Major. It will be a natural minor scale. Include the key signature.

3. Write the natural minor scale in exercise 2, but change it to make it a harmonic minor scale. Include the key signature.

4. This time, change the natural minor scale from exercise 2 to make it a melodic minor scale. Include the key signature.

5. You will be played six scales, A–F. They could be major, natural minor, harmonic minor or melodic minor. First, review CD tracks on pages 26, 70 and 71. Identify them. They will all be played both ascending and descending. Circle your answers below.

A. major natural minor harmonic minor melodic minor

B. major natural minor harmonic minor melodic minor

C. major natural minor harmonic minor melodic minor

D. major natural minor harmonic minor melodic minor

E. major natural minor harmonic minor melodic minor

F. major natural minor harmonic minor melodic minor

Chapter Nine

lesson 4: circle of 5ths
and minor keys

You learned the circle of 5ths and its relationship to the major key signatures on page 49. Here it is again, this time showing the minor keys, as well.

The outside of the circle represents a circle of 5ths (view clockwise). The inside of the circle represents a circle of 4ths (view counterclockwise), which is how it is often viewed by jazz musicians.

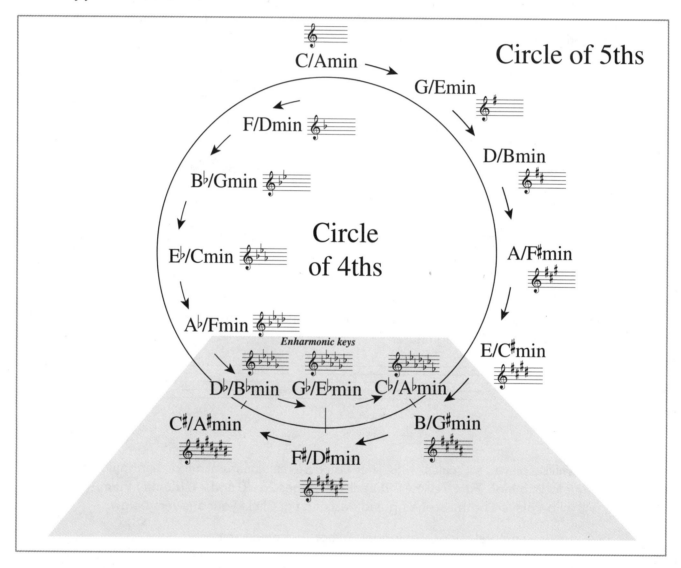

Chapter Ten

lesson 1: sixteenth notes and rests

Vocabulary this page:
sixteenth note/sixteenth rest/double flag/double beam

On pages 12 and 29, you learned the note value tree in $\frac{4}{4}$. You know that when there is a 4 on the bottom of a time signature, a quarter note equals one beat. If a quarter note equals one beat, then an eighth note equals half a beat, a half note equals two beats and a whole note equals four.

Just as we halve the value of a whole note to get half notes, halve the value of a half note to get quarter notes, and halve the value of a quarter note to get eighth notes, we can halve the value of eighth notes to get sixteenth notes. There are two sixteenth notes for each eighth note. So, in $\frac{4}{4}$ time, a sixteenth note equals one fourth of a beat; there are four sixteenth notes in each beat.

A single sixteenth note has a double flag:

Sixteenth notes can be grouped in groups of two or four with double beams.

If there are two sixteenth notes for each eighth note, there are four sixteenth notes for each quarter note, eight sixteenth notes for each half note and sixteen sixteenth notes for each whole note.

Here is an updated version of the note value tree, this time including sixteenth notes.

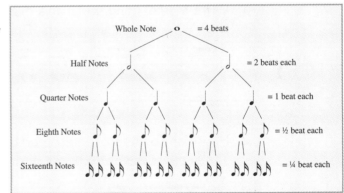

A sixteenth rest looks like this:

For the sake of review, here is a rest value tree.

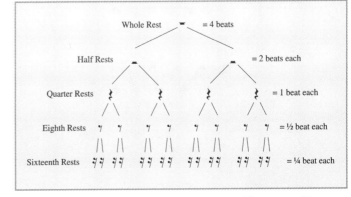

lesson 2: counting sixteenth notes and rests

Vocabulary this page:
preparatory beats

When counting sixteenth notes, we want to verbally subdivide each beat like this: "1-e-&-a, 2-e-&-a, 3-e-&-a, 4-e-&-a." The numbers are the on-beats; the "&s" are the off-beats, and the "e" and "a" fall between them.

1 e & a 2 e & a 3 e & a 4 e & a

Sixteenth notes follow the same rules about stems as half notes and quarter notes: Below the middle line of the staff, stems go up on the right; on or above the third line, stems go down on the left. Also note that sixteenths can be beamed with eighth notes.

Here is an example with counting underneath. It is based on a melody by J.S. Bach. Try to count aloud and clap the rhythm. Hold your hands together on longer notes, take your hands apart on rests. Notice that it is recommended to start subdividing a beat or so before we actually perform eighth or sixteenth notes. These are called preparatory beats. Notice that counting during rests is written in parentheses, and there are x marks under the counts where you would play or clap.

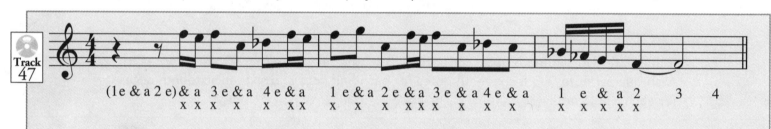

Exercises

1. Write the counting under this music. Use parentheses during rests and x marks to show where notes are played. Do not use preparatory beats.

2. How many beats are represented by the notes and rests to the left of the equal signs? The answers will be numbers, and may include fractions.

A. _____ = _____   B. _____ = _____

C. _____ = _____   D. _____ = _____

Beginning Theory for Adults

lesson 3: interval inversion

Vocabulary this page:
invert/inversion

To invert an interval is to turn it upside down. The bottom note is moved above the upper note, and what was the upper note becomes the new bottom note. When we do this, the name of the interval changes. The new interval number name will be the remainder of 9 minus the original interval number.

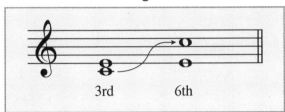

As the example above shows, when inverting a 3rd, subtract 3 from 9 and you get the inverted interval's number name, 6: 9 - 3 = 6. Put another way, the original interval plus the inverted interval always equals 9. Here's a chart of interval inversions (intervals that have been inverted) and an example showing them.

Interval		Inversion		
Unison (1)	+	Octave (8)	=	9
2nd	+	7th	=	9
3rd	+	6th	=	9
4th	+	5th	=	9
5th	+	4th	=	9
6th	+	3rd	=	9
7th	+	2nd	=	9
Octave (8)	+	Unison (1)	=	9

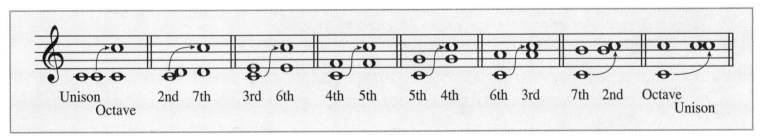

Exercise

Draw the inversions for the intervals and label them with their number names.

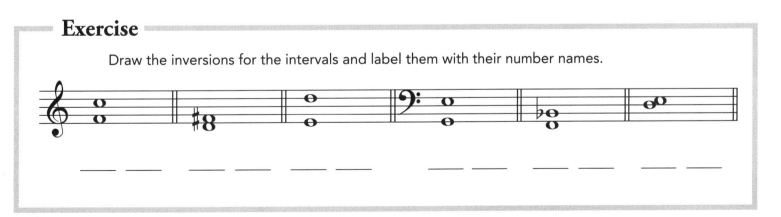

When any interval other than a perfect interval is inverted, its quality name changes, too. For example, an interval that was major becomes minor.

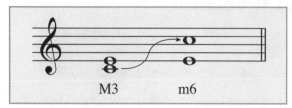

M3   m6

Here is a chart showing what happens to the qualities of intervals when they are inverted, and an example showing them. Notice that, when inverted, a perfect interval remains perfect.

Interval Quality	Inversion Quality
Perfect	Perfect
Major	Minor
Minor	Major
Augmented	Diminished
Diminished	Augmented

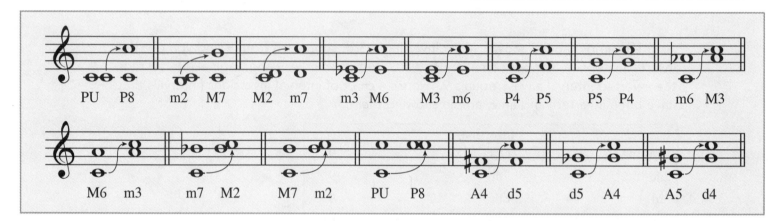

PU   P8   m2   M7   M2   m7   m3   M6   M3   m6   P4   P5   P5   P4   m6   M3

M6   m3   m7   M2   M7   m2   PU   P8   A4   d5   d5   A4   A5   d4

An interval can also be inverted by dropping the top note below the bottom note. All the same rules apply.

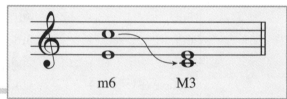

m6   M3

Exercises

1. Draw the inversions for these intervals (by moving the bottom note up) and label the intervals with their number and quality names.

2. Draw the inversions for these intervals (by moving the top note down) and label the intervals with their number and quality names.

Ear Training Exercises

Track 48

1. You will be played two four-measure rhythms on a single note. Fill in the missing rhythms. You'll hear each rhythm twice.

A.

B.

Track 49

2. You will hear six intervals. Identify them with their number and quality names. Use abbreviations.

A._____   B._____   C._____

D._____   E._____   F._____

Track 50

3. You will hear six triads. They will be either major, minor, diminished or augmented. Circle the correct quality for each.

A. major   minor   diminished   augmented
B. major   minor   diminished   augmented
C. major   minor   diminished   augmented
D. major   minor   diminished   augmented
E. major   minor   diminished   augmented
F. major   minor   diminished   augmented

Track 51

4. You will hear three chord progressions, A, B, and C. Listen to the root movement and the chord qualities and draw a line to match them with the correct progression.

A.   I–IV–V–I

B.   I–vi–IV–V

C.   I–ii–V–I

Chapter Ten

lesson 4: close and open position triads

Vocabulary this page:
close position/open position/in the bass /
inversion/inverted triad/1st inversion

So far all of the triads we have seen have been in close position. In other words, the notes were all within one octave; they were spaced as close together as possible. When the notes are spaced over more than one octave, they are in open position.

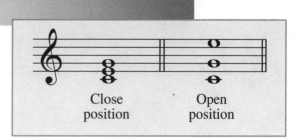

Close position   Open position

lesson 5: triad inversion—1st inversion

On page 57, you learned that any triad that has the root in the bass (on the bottom) is called a root position triad. So far, we have only dealt with root position triads in close position. However, triads can appear in other ways, too.

When a note other than the root is in the bass of a triad, it is called an inversion, or an inverted triad.

If we take the root out of the bass and put it on top of the triad, the 3rd will be in the bass. When the 3rd of the chord is in the bass, it is called 1st inversion. This is true for any type of triad.

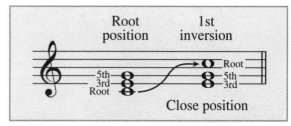

A 1st position triad can be in open position, too. The 3rd is dropped an octave. The notes are the same, but they are arranged differently.

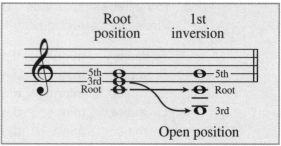

Here are the diatonic triads for the key of C Major in 1st inversion, close position:

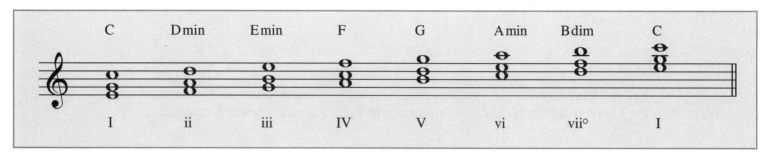

Exercises

1. Draw a rectangle around the 1st inversion triads. Label each chord with a chord symbol on the lines above the staff, and circle the root of each.

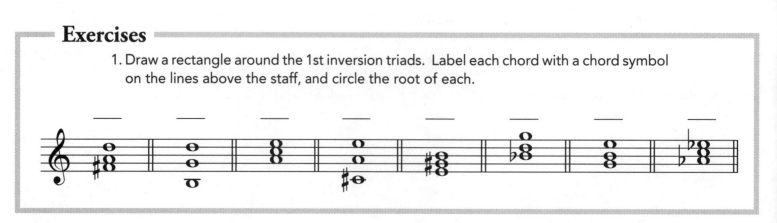

Beginning Theory for Adults

lesson 6: triad inversion—2nd inversion

Vocabulary this page:
2nd inversion

In close position, we can invert the 1st inversion triad again by moving the 3rd to the top, leaving the 5th in the bass. This is called a 2nd inversion triad.

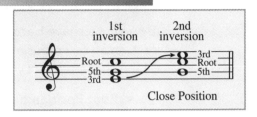

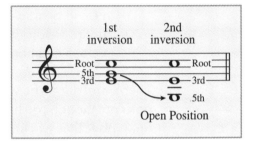

We can also have a 2nd inversion triad in open position, by dropping the 5th into the bass. Any kind of triad can appear in 2nd inversion.

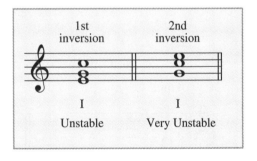

Triads in C Major, 2nd Inversion, Close Position

It is very helpful to notice that in a 1st inversion triad, close position, there is a perfect 4th between the two upper notes (the 5th and the root); in a 2nd inversion triad, there is a perfect 4th between the two lower notes (also the 5th and the root).

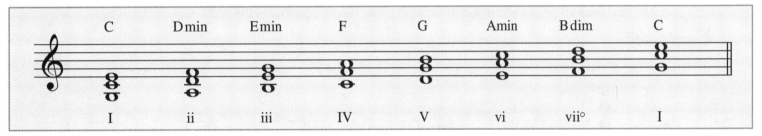

lesson 7: the sounds of inversions

It is also very important to consider how inversions sound. A triad in 1st or 2nd inversion is nowhere near as stable-sounding as a root position triad. For example, even if a C Major chord is the tonic chord (I), it would be very unlikely for a piece in C Major to end on a 1st inversion C Major chord. A 2nd inversion I chord is actually considered to be very unstable, and may even function as a dominant chord (the 5th of the I chord is the same as the root of V), so it is even more unlikely that a piece in C Major would end on a 2nd inversion C Major chord.

Listen to this series of chords, and focus on the relative unstable character of the inversions as compared to the root position chords.

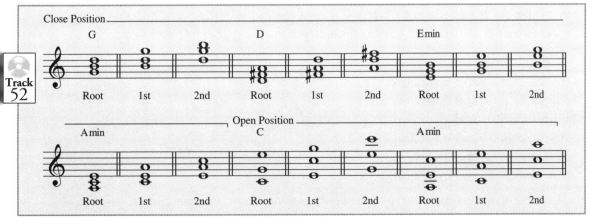

Analyzing Triads in Inversions and Open Positions

By now, you have become accustomed to seeing root position triads in close position. At first, it can be confusing to see them in different inversions and positions. Here is a review of the characteristics you already know that can be helpful when trying to figure out triads:

- Root Position triads have the root in the bass
- 1st inversion triads have the 3rd in the bass
  In close position, there is a 4th between the top two notes.
- 2nd inversion triads have the 5th in the bass
  In close position, there is a 4th between the bottom two notes.

There are different ways to arrange a chord in open position, though you haven't seen many yet. The trick is to remember that you must first figure out which note in the chord is the root. Sometimes, if it isn't obvious, the best thing to do is remember that a triad is three notes stacked in 3rds. Then you can think of the notes as you would a "jumble puzzle" or anagram; as in "Unscramble these letters to create a word: icsum" (= music). For example, if you see these notes, from bottom to top—F, D, A—you can try them in different orders until you find an order arranged in 3rds: D, F, A. Now you know the root is D.

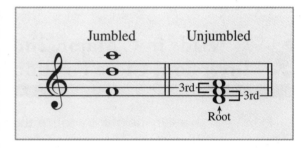

Exercises

1. Label these triads as R (for root position), 1st (for 1st inversion) or 2nd (for 2nd inversion) as appropriate.

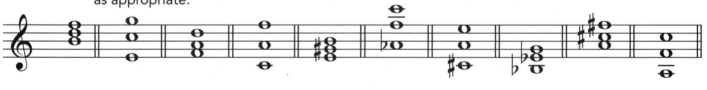

2. Rewrite these triads to invert as indicated.

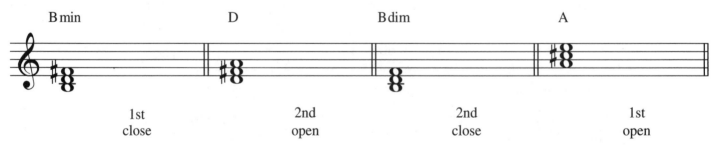

3. Listen to each of the six triads played on the CD and decide whether it is in root position, 1st inversion or 2nd inversion. Circle the correct answers. Each triad will be played two times.

Track 53

A. Root	1st inversion	2nd inversion
B. Root	1st inversion	2nd inversion
C. Root	1st inversion	2nd inversion
D. Root	1st inversion	2nd inversion
E. Root	1st inversion	2nd inversion
F. Root	1st inversion	2nd inversion

Chapter Eleven

lesson 1: eighth-note triplets

Vocabulary this page:
triplet

A *triplet* is three notes played in the time of two. The most common triplet is the eighth note triplet, which is three eighth notes played in the time of two eighth notes (one beat). In an eighth note triplet, the three eighth notes are written under one beam, and there is a figure "3" above or below the notes.

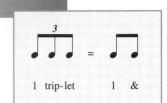

Count aloud, evenly, "1-trip-let, 2-trip-let, 3-trip-let, 4-trip-let." You just counted a measure full of eighth-note triplets.

Dividing each beat into three parts is easy. The tricky part is alternating between regular eighth notes and triplet eighth notes. To do this, one must focus on the time one beat takes, and learn to alternate between dividing that time into two parts and dividing it into three parts. Listen to this counting and clapping example on the CD and then play it back again, this time joining in.

Here is a melody in triplets by J. S. Bach.

lesson 2: dotted eighth notes

Just as you can increase the value of a half note or quarter note by one half by adding a dot, you can increase the value of an eighth note by one half by adding a dot. Since half the value of an eighth note is equal to a sixteenth note, a dotted eighth note is equal to three sixteenth notes. Dotted eighth notes are most often followed by a sixteenth note, and the two note values together equal one beat. The two note values are beamed together.

Here is a rhythm with dotted-eighth/sixteenth rhythms. Counting is included below the staff. Notice the x marks to show where notes are played.

Exercises

1. To the right of the equal sign, write the sum of the values of the notes that are to the left of the equal sign.

A.  = _____

B. = _____

C. = _____

D. = _____

E. = _____

2. Circle the measure that has too many beats.

3. You will hear four rhythms on the CD, A, B, C and D. Draw a line to connect the letter with the correct rhythm.

A.

B.

C.

D.

4. You will be played two four-measure rhythms on a single note. Fill in the missing rhythms.

A.

B.

lesson 3: the V7 chord

Vocabulary this page:
♭7/dominant 7th/major-minor 7th

As you know, the dominant chord (V), of all the triads in a given key, has the strongest tendency to move to the tonic (I) (see pages 64-65). This is because V contains the leading tone (the 7th degree of the major scale of the key) and because of the downward root movement by 5th in the V to I progression. The V7 chord is often used instead of V, and arguably has an even stronger attraction to I.

The "7" in V7 is a minor 7th interval above the root of the chord. Adding this tone (in jazz lingo, referred to as the *flat-7*, ♭7) creates a four-note chord called a *dominant 7th*—sometimes called a *major-minor 7th* chord—that has a major triad with an additional minor 3rd stacked on top.

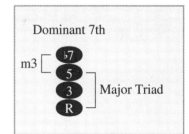

The additional attraction to I comes from the sound of the 7th; in many contexts, our ears are conditioned to hear this tone resolve downward by half step to the 3rd of the tonic chord.

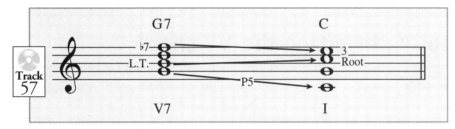

In traditional classical harmony, we only see dominant 7th chords on V. That is the only place in the key where this chord is diatonic. In other words, when you build a four-note chord on V, this is the type of chord that results. This does not happen on any other chord in a major key. Four-note chords on the other scale degrees are also 7th chords, but not of the dominant variety.

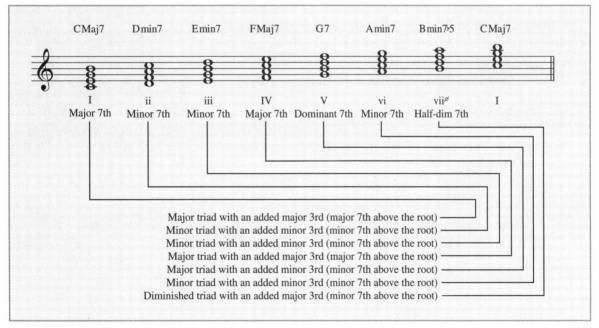

In contexts other than traditional classical harmony, we do not have the same expectations. In blues and rock, the "dominant sound" is so popular that notes in the key will be altered so that I and IV are also dominant 7th chords. In some songs, dominant 7th-type chords will be played on almost any root.

Here the chords used in a typical blues tune in C. Notice that only the V7 does not require an accidental.

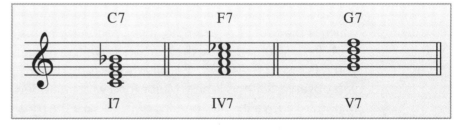

Chapter Eleven

1. Turn these major triads into dominant 7th chords, writing the new chord to the right of the original triad. Use accidentals as necessary.

2. You will hear 6 chords, A-F, on the CD. They will either be major or minor triads or dominant 7th chords. Circle the correct chord type for each.

Track 58

A. major   minor   dominant 7th
B. major   minor   dominant 7th
C. major   minor   dominant 7th
D. major   minor   dominant 7th
E. major   minor   dominant 7th
F. major   minor   dominant 7th

lesson 4: inverting the V7 chord

Just as any triad can be inverted, so too can a four-note chord such as a dominant 7th be inverted. The process is exactly the same, except a four-note chord can be inverted three times.

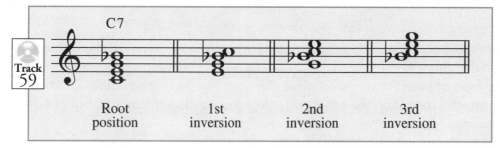

Track 59

| Root position | 1st inversion | 2nd inversion | 3rd inversion |

The root position 7th chord has the root in the bass.
The 1st inversion 7th chord has the 3rd in the bass.
The 2nd inversion 7th chord has the 5th in the bass.
The 3rd inversion 7th chord has the 7th in the bass.

In close position, inverting the 7th chord causes there to be an interval of a major 2nd between the 7th and the root. In 1st inversion, the 2nd is between the top two notes. In 2nd inversion, the 2nd is between the middle two notes. In 3rd inversion, the 2nd is between the bottom two notes.

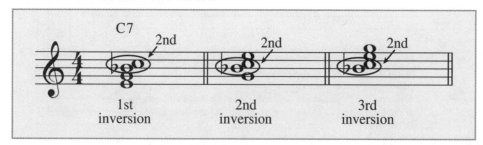

| 1st inversion | 2nd inversion | 3rd inversion |

If you see a four-note chord, it may very well be a 7th chord. You can use the same trick to find the root of a 7th chord that you learned at the top of page 82, but you must now stack four notes in 3rds to discover which is the root. For example, if you see these notes, E♭–A–F–C, you can stack them in 3rds, which will get you this result: F–A–C–E♭. F is clearly the root. Now, if you observe that this is an F Major triad with an added minor 3rd above the 5th, or minor 7 (♭7) above the root, you will know this is an F7 chord.

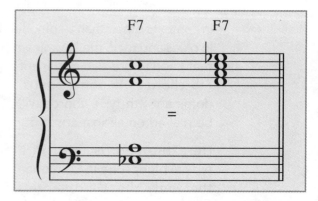

lesson 5: the behavior of a dominant 7th chord

In traditional diatonic harmony, a dominant 7th chord is inherently unstable ... it demands to go somewhere ... to resolve. This is because of the diminished 5th, or tritone, between the 3rd and the 7th of the chord. It is this dissonant interval in the chord that demands resolution, usually to the I chord (tonic). This is true regardless of the inversion.

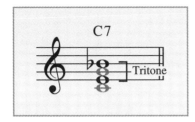

Here is how a V7 chord resolves to I:

- The 7th will descend a half step to the 3rd of I

- The 3rd, which is the leading tone in the key, will ascend a half step to the root of I, the tonic of the key.

- The root of the dominant 7th will descend a 5th or ascend a 4th, also to the root of I.

- Notice that neither the 5th of the V7 chord or the 5th of the tonic chord play an important role in this progression. This voice is often left out of chord voicings.

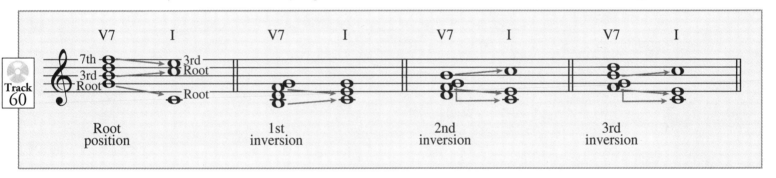

This topic, chord function in diatonic harmony, is a fascinating area of study, and central to becoming a good, knowledgeable musician. If you have followed this discussion, you have already accomplished a great deal. This achievement will forever alter the way you hear music. There's lots more to learn about this, so you can look forward to much more, hopefully always joyful, exploration of harmony.

Answer Key

Page 8

1. A. Higher   B. Lower   C. Higher   D. Lower
2. B.

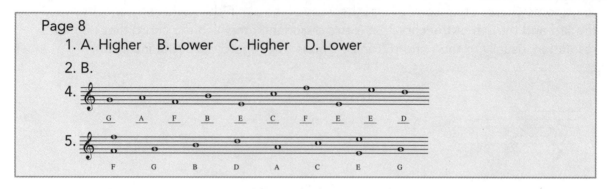

4. G A F B E C F E D

5. F G B D A C E G

Page 10

1. A. Descending   B. Ascending   C. Ascending   D. Descending

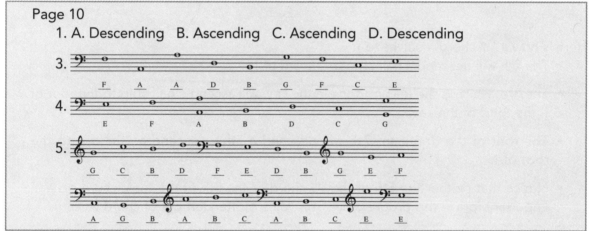

3. F A D B G F C E

4. E F A B D C G

5. G C B D F E D B G E F

   A G B A B C A B C E E

Page 11

1.  ♩ + ♩ = �half
2. ♩ + ♩ + ♩ + ♩ = ○
3. ♩half + ♩half = ○
4. 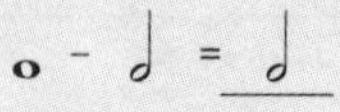 ○ − ♩half = ♩half

Page 13

1. A.  ♩ + ♩half = __2__   B. ♩half + ♩half = __4__   C. ♩ + ♩half = __3__
2. A. 3   B. quarter

3.

4.

Page 14

1. A. ▬ + ▬ = __4__   B. 𝄽 + ▬ = __3__   C. ▬ + 𝄽 = __5__

2.

Page 15

1. 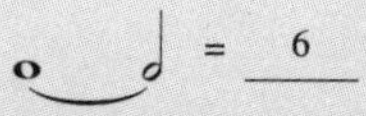 ○ ⌣ ♩half = __6__   2.  ♩half ⌣ ♩ = __3__

3. ♩ ⌣ ♩ = __2__   4. ○ ⌣ ♩ = __5__

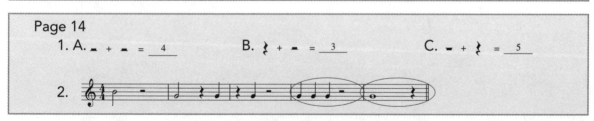

Beginning Theory for Adults

Page 17

1.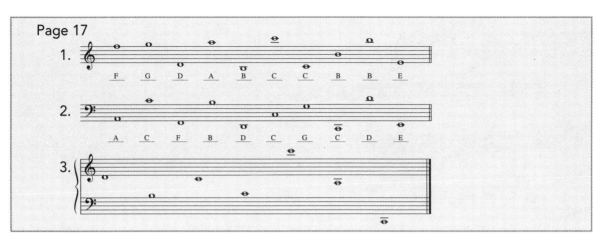
F G D A B C C B B E

2. A C F B D C G C D E

3.

Page 18

1.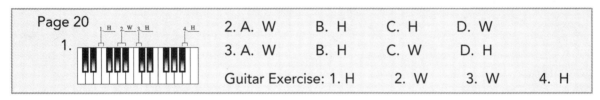
Close Far Close Far Close Far Close Far Close Far

2. A. Far   B. Close   C. Close   D. Far

Page 20

1.

2. A. W   B. H   C. H   D. W

3. A. W   B. H   C. W   D. H

Guitar Exercise: 1. H   2. W   3. W   4. H

Page 23

4.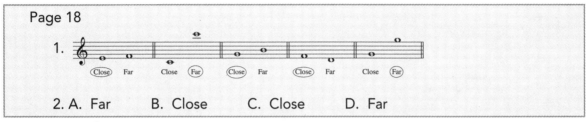
F F# F# F# G G Gb Gb G F# E F# F# A A

Page 27

1. A. Major B. Chromatic C. Chromatic D. Major

2. A. Major B. Other C. Major D. Chromatic E. Other F. Major

3. A. 2 B. 1 C. 3 D. 4

   E. 2 F. 4 G. 1 H. 3

Page 28

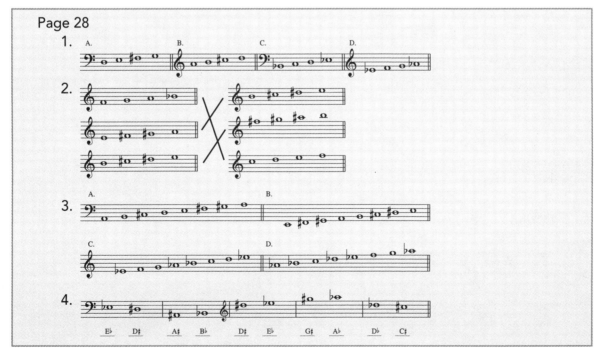

Eb D# A# Bb D# Eb G# Ab Db C#

Page 32

Page 38

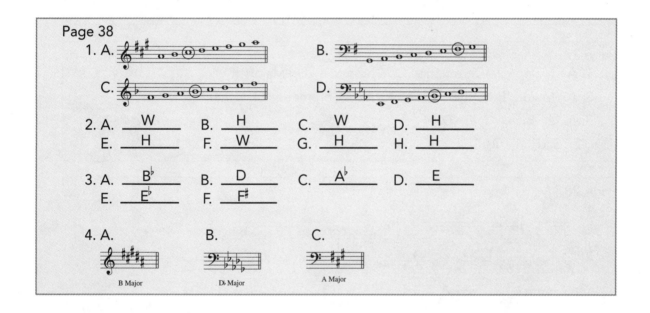

Page 41

1. A. even   B. odd   C. odd
   D. odd   E. even   F. even

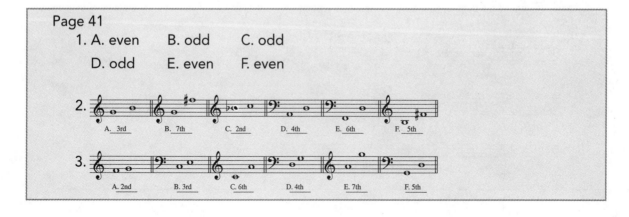

Beginning Theory for Adults

Page 42

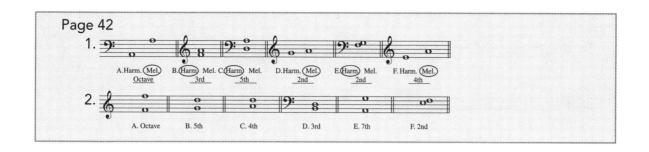

1.
A. Harm. (Mel.) — Octave
B. (Harm) Mel. — 3rd
C. (Harm) Mel. — 5th
D. Harm. (Mel.) — 2nd
E. (Harm) Mel. — 2nd
F. Harm. (Mel.) — 4th

2.
A. Octave
B. 5th
C. 4th
D. 3rd
E. 7th
F. 2nd

Page 46

1. A. P5   B. M2   C. M2   D. P5   E. P5   F. M2
2. A. M3   B. M7   C. M3   D. M7   E. M3   F. M3
3. A. P4   B. M7   C. M7   D. P4   E. P4   F. M7
4. A. P8   B. P8   C. M6   D. M6   E. P8   F. M6
5. A. M2   B. M3   C. M3   D. M2   E. M3   F. M2
6. A. M6   B. M7   C. M6   D. M6   E. M7   F. M7

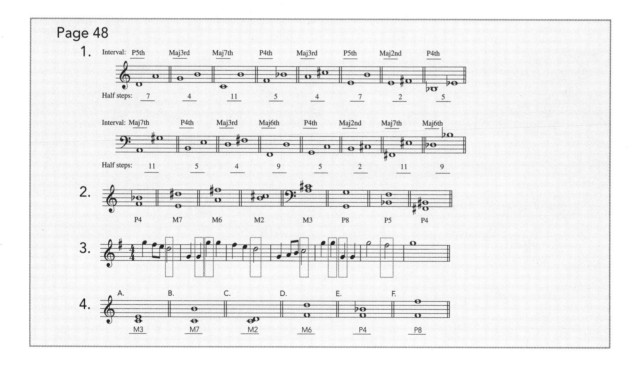

7. M2   M6   P8   P4   M3   P5   P4   M7

Page 48

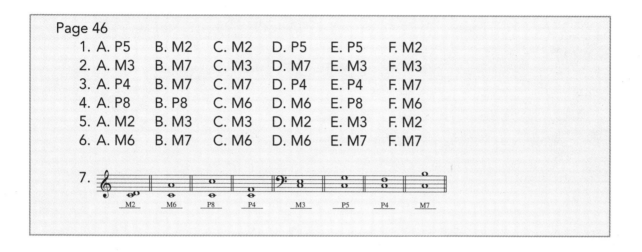

1. Interval: P5th, Maj3rd, Maj7th, P4th, Maj3rd, P5th, Maj2nd, P4th
Half steps: 7, 4, 11, 5, 4, 7, 2, 5

Interval: Maj7th, P4th, Maj3rd, Maj6th, P4th, Maj2nd, Maj7th, Maj6th
Half steps: 11, 5, 4, 9, 5, 2, 11, 9

2. P4   M7   M6   M2   M3   P8   P5   P4

3.

4. A. M3   B. M7   C. M2   D. M6   E. P4   F. P8

Page 50

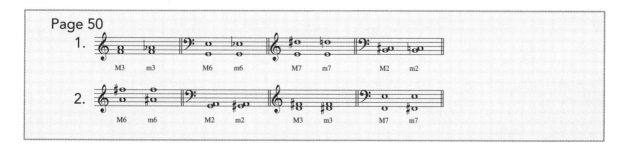

1. M3 m3   M6 m6   M7 m7   M2 m2

2. M6 m6   M2 m2   M3 m3   M7 m7

Page 52

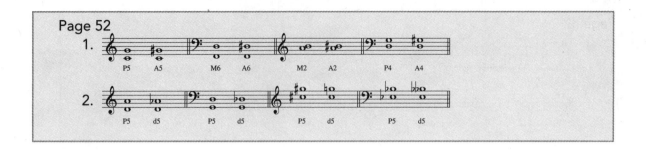

Page 53

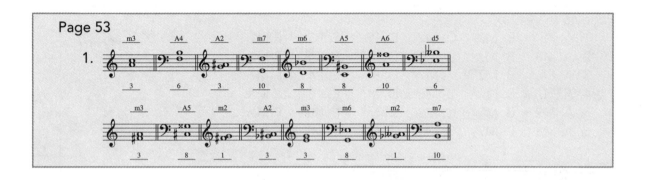

Page 56

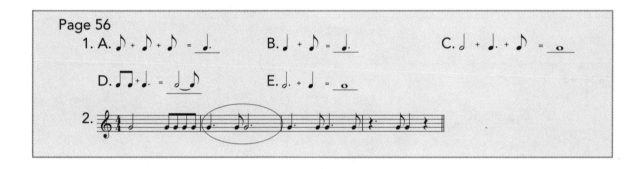

Page 57

Page 58

3. A. Major   B. Minor   C. Minor   D. Major   E. Major   F. Minor

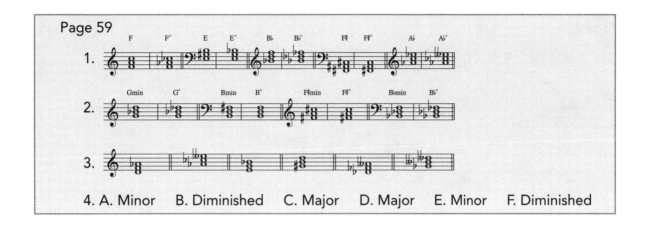

Page 59

4. A. Minor   B. Diminished   C. Major   D. Major   E. Minor   F. Diminished

Page 60

3. A. Major   B. Augmented   C. Minor   D. Diminished   E. Minor   F. Augmented

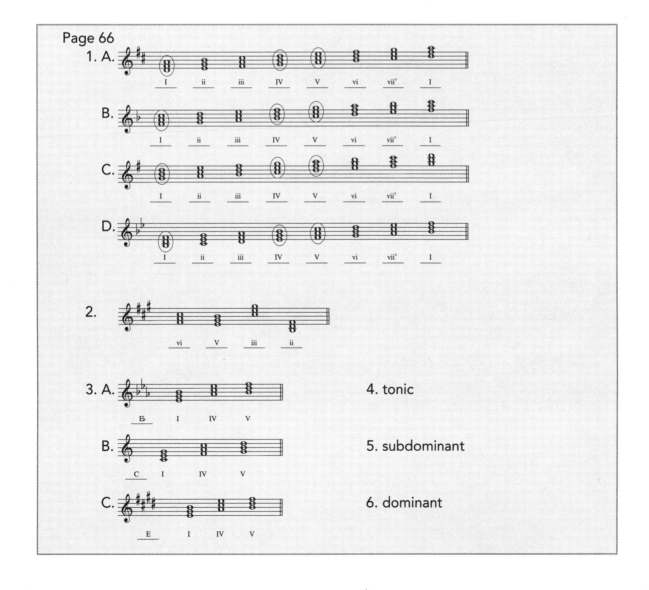

Page 66

4. tonic

5. subdominant

6. dominant

Page 68

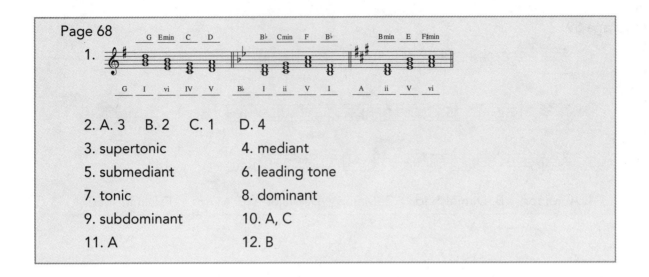

2. A. 3   B. 2   C. 1   D. 4

3. supertonic

4. mediant

5. submediant

6. leading tone

7. tonic

8. dominant

9. subdominant

10. A, C

11. A

12. B

Page 69

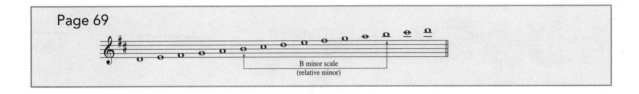

Page 73

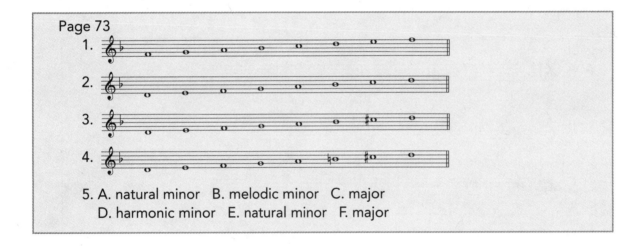

5. A. natural minor   B. melodic minor   C. major
   D. harmonic minor   E. natural minor   F. major

Page 76

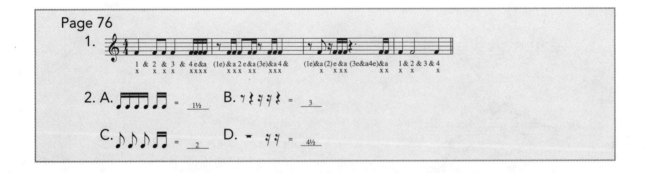

Page 77

5th | 4th | 3rd | 6th | 7th | 2nd | 6th | 3rd | 4th | 5th | 2nd | 7th

Page 78

1.

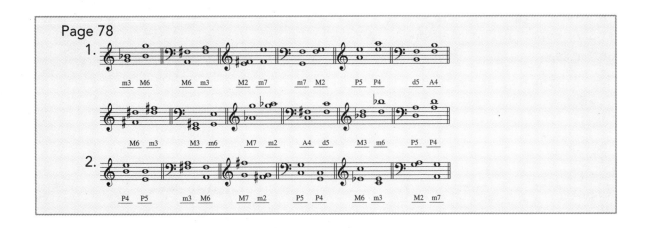

m3 | M6 | M6 | m3 | M2 | m7 | m7 | M2 | P5 | P4 | d5 | A4

M6 | m3 | M3 | m6 | M7 | m2 | A4 | d5 | M3 | m6 | P5 | P4

2.

P4 | P5 | m3 | M6 | M7 | m2 | P5 | P4 | M6 | m3 | M2 | m7

Page 79

1. A.

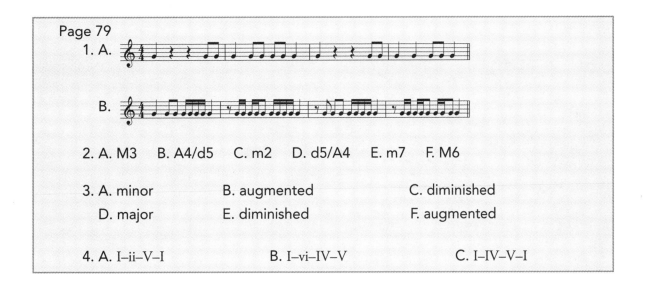

B.

2. A. M3   B. A4/d5   C. m2   D. d5/A4   E. m7   F. M6

3. A. minor   B. augmented   C. diminished

   D. major   E. diminished   F. augmented

4. A. I–ii–V–I   B. I–vi–IV–V   C. I–IV–V–I

Page 80

1.

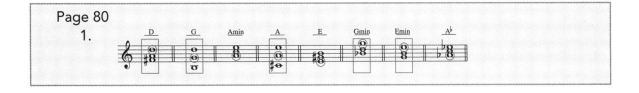

Page 82

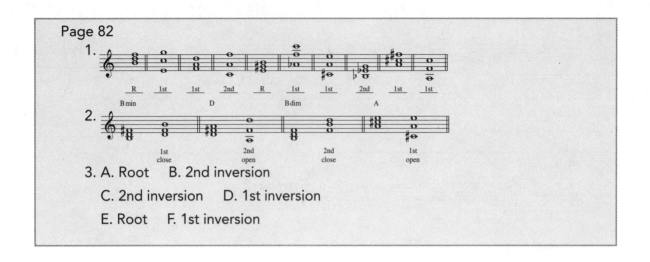

3. A. Root   B. 2nd inversion

C. 2nd inversion   D. 1st inversion

E. Root   F. 1st inversion

Page 84

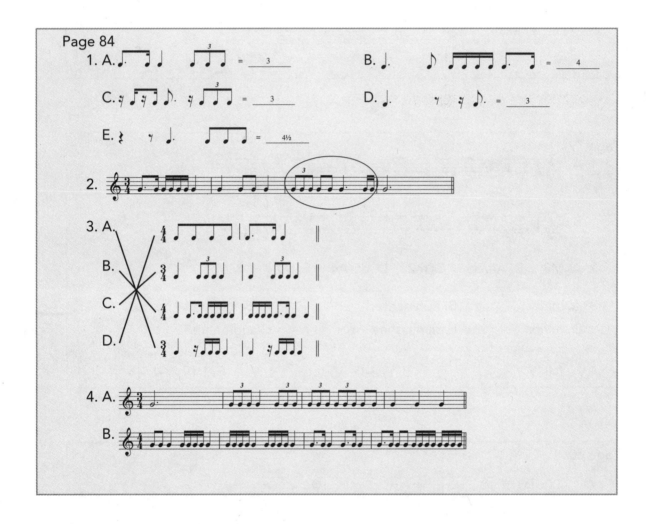

Page 86

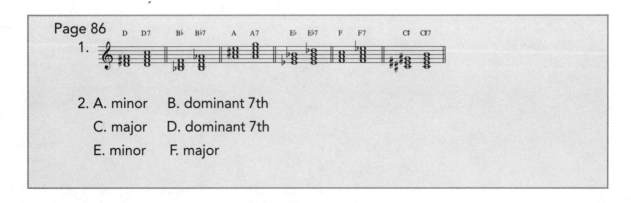

2. A. minor   B. dominant 7th

C. major   D. dominant 7th

E. minor   F. major

Beginning Theory for Adults